BYRON AS SKEPTIC AND BELIEVER

BYRON AS SKEPTIC AND BELIEVER

BY

EDWARD WAYNE MARJARUM

NEW YORK / RUSSELL & RUSSELL

PREFATORY NOTE

This study of Byron was a dissertation presented to the faculty of Princeton University in candidacy for the degree of Doctor of Philosophy, and was accepted by the Department of English in April, 1931. Since that time, minor revisions have been necessary in the light of recent works on Byron, but there has been no essential modification.

Valuable suggestions in the preparation of this study came to me from Professor Robert Scoon. The encouragement of Professor Paul Elmer More and the suggestions of Professor Thomas M. Parrott and of Professor G. H. Gerould were also most helpful. The untiring patience and the generous assistance of J. Duncan Spaeth, formerly Professor of English at Princeton University and now President of the University of Kansas City, under whose direction the work was done, have imposed an obligation which formal acknowledgement can only in part discharge.

For permission to reproduce copyrighted material from Byron's verse and prose, the author wishes to acknowledge his indebtedness to John Murray, of London, and to Charles Scribner's Sons, New York. Similar permission was granted by Covici Friede, Inc., New York. Further acknowledgement for permission to quote from Paul Elmer More came from The Atlantic Monthly Publishing Company and from Houghton Mifflin Company, Boston, publishers of the Cambridge edition of Byron.

                                                            E. W. M.

ERRATA

Page	Line	Correction
5	25	supposAJitious to supposititious
5	29	theories in Cain to theories in Cain
5	n. 19 l. 2	deity to Deity
5	n. 19 l. 4	to read p. 41 (1816); Letters, V, etc.
6	n. 23 l. 7	Adios! to Adios'
7	7	divine to Divine
10	10	(1816) to (1818)
12	n. 43 l. 5	entire line to be omitted
13	2	Unitary to unitary
14	n. 53 l. 2	do, Letters to do,' Letters
21	n. 76	(1922) to (1822)
24	n. 4 l. 2	ètat to état
29	39	aftereffect to after effect
39	17	This to This
53	10	method does to methods do
56	30	Love to love
58	n. 35 l. 1	Manfred to Manfred
62	20	semipantheist's to semi-pantheist's

TABLE OF CONTENTS

I N T R O D U C T I O N

During one of Byron's occasional spells of diary-keeping he wrote, 'This journal is a relief. When I am tired--as I generally am--out comes this, and down goes every thing. But I can't read it over; and God knows what contradictions it may contain. If I am sincere with myself (but I fear one lies more to one's self than to any one else), every page should confute, refute, and utterly abjure its predecessor.'[1]

Byron's disregard for consistency is not a sign of intellectual irresponsibility. Despite all his flippancy, despite all the errors of judgment into which he was led by an intellect remarkable for its vigor rather than its profundity, there is evident in all that he wrote a love of truth which only superficial criticism can ignore. A faithful representation of his thoughts necessarily presupposed contradictions; 'if I am sincere with myself,' inconsistencies must follow as the night the day. His very contradictions grow out of that 'proud sincerity' which Mr. Paul Elmer More recognizes as the basis of his character.[2]

Although Byron was perfectly aware of his instability of opinion, he did not cultivate paradox for drawing-room consumption in the fashion of Oscar Wilde. He made no pretense to consistency because he considered himself to have a dual personality. He was once examined by a phrenologist--'a discoverer of faculties and dispositions from the heads. . . . He says all mine are strongly marked, but very antithetical, for every thing developed in or on this same scull of mine has its opposite in great force, so that, to believe him, my good and evil are at perpetual war. . . .'[3] At his very worst, Byron's duality approaches the pathological;[4] at his

[1]Byron, Letters, II, 366.
[2]P. E. More, Complete Poetical Works of Lord Byron, 'Biographical Sketch,' p. xii: 'For one thing the basis of his character was undoubtedly a proud sincerity, yet his acts and words wore often the appearance of sham. To discriminate between that sincerity and that sham, and to show how they were related, would be as rich an exercise of psychology as a man might desire.'
[3]Letters, III, 137 (1814).
[4]Blessington, p. 103: 'You will believe me, what I sometimes believe myself, mad, when I tell you that I seem to have two states of existence.' Cf. ibid, p. 352: 'I am so changeable, being everything by turns and

best, in the resolute fidelity of Don Juan to the multiform
aspects of human experience, the panoramic sweep of Byron's vision could not be brought within a nicely proportioned per-
spective. Arnold has called attention to 'the promiscuous
adoption of all the matter offered to the poet by life, just
as it was offered, without thought or patience for the mysteri-
ous transmutation to be operated on this matter by poetic
form.'[5] If Byron had no synthesis to expound, no gospel to
promulgate, it was not merely because he lacked constructive
vision; his unflinching honesty recognized more things in
heaven and earth than he could bring within the compass of a
single philosophy.

> But if a writer should be quite consistent,
> How could he possibly show things existent?
>   Don Juan, xv, st. 87.

Mr. Desmond MacCarthy has pointed out that to write
directly from the mood of the moment is a kind of sincerity
to be distinguished from that which adheres steadily to fixed
beliefs, and that Byron's poetry secures its directness and
force from that kind of sincerity.[6] It is from this point of
view that one should approach Byron. It may be objected that
he has no greater claim upon the patience of the logically-
minded than other poets, and must stand or fall upon the
usual criteria; but sound criticism must first get understanding, and failure to recognize the peculiar nature of
Byron's sincerity can lead only to erroneous judgments.

In investigating the backgrounds of Byron's poetry
one is often likely to recall Goethe's dictum, 'sobald er
reflectirt ist er ein Kind.' With due allowance for over-
statement, and for the intellectual disparity between Goethe
and Byron, it must be conceded that Byron was not a profound
or original thinker. To draw from his letters, his journals,
his poetry, and from the records of those who lived and talked
with him, an abstract of his beliefs is not to contribute a
noteworthy chapter to the history of thought.

On the other hand, there are in Byron qualities which
have engaged the attention of the ablest critics and of the
most painstaking artists. Mazzini, Swinburne, Arnold, Shelley,
Goethe--a poet who can command praise from such as these may

---

nothing long,—I am such a strange mélange of good and evil, that it would
be difficult to describe me.' See also Don Juan, xvii, st. 11:

> So that I almost think that the same skin
> For one without--has two or three within.

[5]Matthew Arnold, Essays in Criticism, p. 184.
[6]Desmond MacCarthy, 'Byron: Man and Poet,' p. 845.

be called great. Where lies the secret of his power? There
are many answers, perhaps all of them in some measure right;
but Swinburne's familiar judgment--'the splendid and imperishable excellence of sincerity and strength'--seems to
come nearest. There is in Byron a challenging vigor, a relentless longing to

                            comprehend
        The wondrous architecture of the world,
        And measure every wandering planet's course,
        Still climbing after knowledge infinite,
        And always moving as the restless spheres.

        Byron's passionate curiosity must be sympathetically
understood in order to interpret his poetry. His speculations are in themselves worth little; but in so far as they
aid in the interpretation of his poetry they may be worth
much. And in the case of Byron there is no department of
thought which by its relationships and ramifications is so
representative of his intellectual activity as his ceaseless
reflection upon the nature and value of human experience, and
the significance of the traditional beliefs by which man has
for ages sought to interpret his experience. Byron was highly sensitive to any hint of the supernatural, and hence deeply concerned with doubt and belief. Religious prepossess-
sions had a determining influence upon his scientific, historic, and philosophical interests, and because of the implications which such interests had upon matters of doubt and
belief they became an integral part of his poetry.

        My music has some mystic diapasons;
        And there is much which could not be appreciated
        In any manner by the uninitiated.
                                    Don Juan, xiv, st. 22

        The present study traces four recurrent themes, some-
times approaching a temporary agreement, at other times dia-
metrically opposing one another, always appearing in a state
of bewildering confusion, which supplant one another and are
in turn disavowed, only to be championed as passionately the
next hour. Calvinism, Skepticism, Naturalism, and Roman
Catholicism, not avowed in any definite formulas or repre-
senting an ordered sequence of intellectual development, but
reflected in the shifting hues of a 'versified aurora borealis,' constitute major interests of his thought and the main
region of his song.
        Critical estimates of Byron's poetry require far
greater familiarity with the man apart from his works than
in the case of most other English poets. Although his critical theory was neoclassical, his practice was romantic; he
abandoned the comparatively impersonal tone of Pope for the

confessional note of Rousseau. Notably weak as a dramatist, Byron was most at ease in the picaresque narrative interspersed with reflective digressions. Scott, although comparable to Byron as a romantic narrative poet, was creative rather than self-expressive, in the sense that his works portray imaginative experience objectively; Byron was self-expressive, that is, concerned with his own experience. His passionate concern with religious questions is constantly reflected as a poetic motif; it is therefore necessary to take into account all that can be learned of his intellectual development, even in fields apart from literature.

Among the more important continental discussions of Byron's relation to the thought of his times is the brilliant critique by Georg Brandes. His treatment of Byron shows, however, a prepossession with Byron's significance as a radical poet; he therefore places particular emphasis on Byron's skepticism, but is less concerned with the inner conflict arising from Byron's departures from orthodox beliefs. For the purposes of literary criticism, considered for the moment as distinct from literary history, the chief importance of Byron's skepticism is its effect upon his psychology.

Two special studies of Byron's poetry in fields related to his religious difficulties have thus far appeared. The earlier, J. O. E. Donner's Lord Byrons Weltanschauung (1897), still has great value, but is in some respects inadequate. Donner does not render easily available the supplementary evidence to be found in Byron's prose. He pays scant attention to the profound effect of Calvinistic training on Byron, and even less to the later tendency toward Catholicism. The title of his work shows the chief difference between his point of view and that outlined in the foregoing pages. Donner seeks to trace the development of a deistic Weltanschauung in Byron's poetry by reconciling as best he can the poet's contradictory statements of belief. Few subsequent critics have accepted Donner's conclusions; there is rather a general agreement that Byron never systematized his ideas and therefore cannot be said to have a Weltanschauung. The contrarieties of Byron's conflicting opinions can not be reconciled; a careful sifting brings some order out of the confusion, but only by recognizing the duality of Byron's mind.

A later study is Manfred Eimer's Byron und der Kosmos. Here also there is an attempt to infer the changes in Byron's point of view toward the world. The emphasis is placed upon Byron's acquaintance with theories of astronomy and cosmogony; from a careful compilation of all the prose and poetry reflecting Byron's interests in these fields, Eimer reaches the conclusion that Byron's final belief was 'cosmic deism.' Eimer has quite properly excluded from his study purely theological aspects of Byron's thought, and those not called into play by scientific interests. The persistence of Calvinistic influences and the changing attitude toward Catholicism are without the scope of his study. But aside from this special characteristic, Eimer's conclusions are open to some question. He believes that the theories of natural science enabled Byron to overcome the confusion of his ideas and raised his spirits from their habitual depression. Eimer departs from the consensus of critical opinion, that the poet of Don Juan is still embittered, and that for the heroics of Manfred he has substituted mocking laughter. He attributes to Byron a fixity of opinion irreconcilable with the alert skepticism of Don Juan. Eimer's interpretation of Byron's poetry was probably modified by the special nature of his evidence; but his investigation has enduring value in the illumination of an important aspect of Byron frequently overlooked. He has added a cubit to our estimate of Byron's stature.

The present study makes no attempt to establish a single point of view as most representative of Byron's last years. The poetry written during his maturity in Italy reflects his latest beliefs but not final beliefs. To the very last he was receptive to every influence, and inquisitive about all things. Some writers, notably Shelley, exclude from their art the discordant and incongruous; the world is imaged in their poetry in idealized form. They find reality in the world of the spirit, and eliminate everything else. There are also poets who, like Goethe, seek to embrace all the multifarious stuff of existence, and to subdue it to the proportions of their art. Byron belonged to neither class. No single aspect of his genius was dominant; hence there is no evidence in his poetry of a consistent philosophy attained as the result of an orderly development. Had he depended like Wordsworth on the inspiration of steady progress through days 'bound each to each in natural piety,' much of his best poetry would never have been written. Byron's art did not grow out of his progress, but out of the tumult of warring elements within him. Conflict was the essence of his experience and the permanent inspiration of his poetry.

> All life is motion; and
> In life commotion is the extremest point
> Of life.
>> Deformed Transformed, I.ii.591-593.

Chapter One

DOCTRINAL CHRISTIANITY

Yet I wish well to Trojan and to Tyrian,
For I was bred a moderate Presbyterian.
                    Don Juan, xv, st. 91.

When Don Juan set out from Ismail to bear the news of
victory to the Empress Catherine, he was accompanied by the
little Turkish girl whom the exigencies of battle had left
under his protection. With a kindly interest in her welfare,
he permitted the church to attempt her conversion; but 'the
little Turk refused to be converted.' She was born and bred
a Moslem, and no subsequent teaching could move her.

'T was strange enough she should retain the
                    impression
Through such a scene of change, and dread, and
                    slaughter;
But though three bishops told her the transgression,
She show'd a great dislike to holy water.
                    Don Juan, x, st. 56 (1822).

The story of Leila's obstinacy reflects something more
personal than wit. From Byron's own experience he had learned
that beliefs acquired in childhood leave an indelible impression. 'It is not a matter of volition to unbelieve,' he told
Medwin. 'Who likes to own that he has been a fool all his
life,--to unlearn all that he has been taught in his youth?'[1]
All his life Byron was conscious of the inability of
the mind to shake off feelings regularly associated during
childhood with any train of thought. A man who has been
'cudgelled to Church for the first ten years of [his] life'
can hardly be expected to recall the period with pleasure.[2]

[1]Medwin, p. 51 (1821-2). Cf. Childe Harold, iv, st. 76 (1818); cf.
Blessington, p. 315: 'perhaps the greatest of all are the impressions
made on our minds in early youth. . . .impressions which have such weight
in deciding our future opinions'; ibid., p. 112: 'first impressions are
indelible' (1823). See also Letters, V, 490: 'who can say, I will believe. . . .?' (1821).
[2]Letters, II, 222 (1813). For the story of Byron's early training in
religion by May Gray and Scottish Presbyterian schoolmasters see Moore's
Life, Chaps.I, II, and III, and Letters, V, 406-7. A penetrating account
of these early influences, based on shrewd conjecture rather than full

But despite Byron's consequent aversion to traditional observances, he was always acutely sensitive about religious
beliefs. By the time he was nineteen he claimed to have read
Blair, Porteus, Tillotson, and Hooker.[3] He found them 'tire-
some' and abhorrent; but still he read theology, mastered by
a passionate curiosity which, although it made him no formal
theologian, familiarized him with the main issues of theological controversy.[4]

When Byron returned to Newstead after the first tour
of the Mediterranean, he received long visits from Francis
Hodgson and William Harness, both of whom later became clergy-
men of the Church of England. Harness subsequently wrote,
'Byron, from his early education in Scotland, had been taught
to identify the principles of Christianity with the extreme
dogmas of Calvinism. His mind had thus imbibed a most miserable prejudice, which appeared to be the only obstacle to his
hearty acceptance of the Gospel. Of this error we were most
anxious to disabuse him.'[5]

By 'the extreme dogmas of Calvinism' Harness meant
the great emphasis laid upon original sin and predestination
in Calvinistic systems, doctrines which exercised a profound
influence upon Byron's imagination. The fascination which
they held for him explains in large measure his life-long concern with theological controversy.

Harness's account was later confirmed by that of Ana-
belle Milbanke. During the courtship she questioned Byron
about his religious beliefs. He was not at all inclined to
discuss them with her,[6] but replied: 'I now come to a subject

_____

documentary evidence, is given in Maurois's Byron, Chap. III. See also
Letters, V, 391 (1821); ibid., III, 401 ff. (1813).

[3]Hugh Blair (1718-1800) was a Scottish Presbyterian divine and popular
writer of sermons. Beilby Porteus (1731-1808), Bishop of London, noted
as a strict disciplinarian, opposed the Catholic Emancipation Bill of 1805.
John Tillotson (1630-1694), Archbishop of Canterbury, was one of the most
famous divines of his century. Richard Hooker (1553-1600), author of Laws
of Ecclesiastical Polity, has always exercised a profound influence upon
English theology.

[4]Byron's memorandum (Moore, Chap. V) of 'works I have perused' lists
the four theologians named above, followed by the comment, 'all very tire-
some. I abhor books of religion, though I reverence and love my God, without the blasphemous notions of sectaries, or belief in their absurd and
damnable heresies, mysteries, and Thirty-nine Articles.'

[5]Harness, Life of the Rev. Francis Hodgson, I, 219-221. Reprinted in
Letters, I, 179ff.

[6]'Seriously, if she imagines that I particularly delight in canvassing
the creed of St. Athanasius. . . .she will be mistaken.' Letter to Lady
Melbourne, Correspondence, I, 255 (1814).

of your inquiry which you must have perceived I always hither-
to avoided--an awful one--"Religion." I was bred in Scotland
among Calvinists in the first part of my life which gave me a
dislike to that persuasion.'[7] She later discovered that
Byron's dislike was closely related to fear. 'Not merely
from casual expressions,' she wrote, 'but from the whole
tenour of Lord Byron's feelings, I could not but conclude he
was a believer in the inspiration of the Bible, and had the
gloomiest Calvinistic tenets. To that unhappy view of the
relation of the creature to the Creator, I have always ascribed the misery of his life.'[8] Lady Byron was not disposed
to sympathize with him on the score of religion; her inclinations toward Socinianism inspired little sympathetic understanding of that awe of the supernatural which may be induced
in minds like Byron's by Calvinistic beliefs.[9]

Lady Byron's testimony is important as that of an in-
telligent woman speaking from personal knowledge. His 'dislike to that persuasion' is not to be understood as evidence
that he shut out from his mind the teachings of Calvinism.
'The worst of it is,' he told her, 'I do believe.'[10] Realizing, as Lady Byron evidently did, that the poet was acutely
sensitive about religious matters, and that he was tormented
by fears, she immediately recognized in Dr. Kennedy's account
of his conversations on religion with Byron the characteristics of her former husband. 'Dr. Kennedy is most faithful
where you doubt his being so,' she wrote.[11]

The misapprehensions about Byron's character into
which external appearances betrayed those who knew him im-
perfectly were exemplified in the judgments passed by his
associates upon Kennedy's Conversations on Religion with Lord
Byron. His contemporary reputation for irreligion and his
petty eagerness to display in debate an imagined ability in
religious controversy have obscured the true significance of
those discussions.[12] That Byron was so concerned with a

[7]Letters, III, 401 ff. (1813).

[8]Henry Crabb Robinson, Diary, III, 455-6, prints Lady Byron's letter
written to defend the accuracy of James Kennedy's account of Byron's religious beliefs. Reprinted in Letters, VI, 261, note 2.

[9]Byron later told Kennedy that the religion of the Socinians 'seems to
be spreading very much. Lady Byron is a great one among them, and much
looked up to. She and I used to have a great many discussions on religion,
and some of our differences arose from this point. . . .' (Kennedy,
p. 196.) Elze (Chap. VI, pp. 188-190) maintains that Lady Byron's authoritarian dogmatism was the disturbing element in their conversations, and
denies the view here taken. There is no reason to assume that either
view is exclusive of the other.

[10]Letters, VI, 261, note 2.

[11]Loc. cit.

[12]Thus Galt (p. 278) and after him Medwin (p. 256) repeat the rumor

theatrical role in the conversations as not to appreciate
their amusing side is disproved by his own letters.[13] Whether
Kennedy imagined that he was always being taken seriously, or
whether Byron fancied that future generations would be impressed by his learning or his forensic skill, is not important; the significance of the Conversations is to reveal in
Byron a state of mind which is constantly reflected in his
poetry. He hoped that the discussions with Kennedy would
clarify his religious thinking; and he entered into the de-
bates because he was tormented by a confusion of ideas which
he wished to bring into order. Byron's contact with the
Christian tradition occasioned neither settled belief nor mere
indifference. He experienced an inner conflict of which his
constant preoccupation with traditional beliefs is an evidence.

This is not to say that Byron's philosophizing was
static. The skepticism of his youthful period verged in
time toward critical idealism, and the natural religion of
his earliest poetry was later infused with pantheistic beliefs and the spirit of scientific curiosity. But no such
modifications are to be observed in the core of belief which
he acquired from traditional religion, nor is there any essential change in the state of mind with which he approached
theological doctrines. His contact during youth and early
manhood with the orthodox tradition consisted in a series of
experiences to which he attached certain values; and at no
time during life did he change his system of values. His
vacillations between belief and doubt were always attended by
inward distress; religious uncertainty was a constant source
of suffering to him.

One or two exceptions must be made. His very early
poetry is written with an evident assurance of personal and
individual immortality, or at times of bodily resurrection.
These early poems are hence to be understood as orthodox
Christian lyrics.[14] Although evidences of Byron's skepticism
appear in the Prayer of Nature (1806), Byron often returns in
later years to the traditional faith in a personal survival.[15]

---

current among the officers at Missolonghi that Byron engaged in the conversations merely to collect material for a satirical portrait of Don
Juan as a Methodist.

[13]Letters, VI, 271 (1823); ibid., VI, 261-3 (1823); Muir's comment,
ibid., VI, 429-430; and Finlay's "Reminiscences" (Stanhope, p. 499 ff.).

[14]On the Death of a Young Lady (1802); To D—— (1803); Epitaph on a
Friend (1803); A Fragment ('When, to their airy hall,' 1803); To Caroline
(1805) (beginning 'When I hear you'); The Tear (1806); Love's Last Adieu,
V. 37: 'life of probation for rapture divine' (1806). Cf. Donner,
pp. 47-49, for discussion of these poems.

[15]To my Son 11-12 (1807); The Adieu 101-4 (1807); Bright Be the Place
of Thy Soul (1808); To Thyrza 45-56 (1811); Childe Harold, ii, st. 8-9

This early acceptance of orthodoxy finally became to Byron what Christianity, in the words of Taine, became to Goethe, 'remembrance and poetic feeling.'[16] And this is virtually the only modification of Byron's essential attitude toward Christian dogma.

Byron's continued acceptance of some theistic beliefs is of particular importance in view of the charges of atheism often levelled against him, and also with regard to his later interest in pantheistic and materialistic systems of thought. Byron never departed from the belief in a Supreme Being. 'God made man, let us love him,' piped the little Aberdonian at five. 'Devotion is the affection of the heart, and this I feel; for when I view the wonders of creation, I bow to the Majesty of Heaven; and when I feel the enjoyments of life, health, and happiness, I feel grateful to God for having bestowed these upon me.' So Kennedy reports him as saying less than a year before his death.[17] It was the persistence of this core of belief that made him resent so furiously the charges of atheism and irreligion.[18] His assertions of belief and denials of infidelity were both frequent and emphatic.[19] Even when the theories of geologists seemed to conflict with Genesis, as in the writings of Cuvier, Byron saw no ground for skepticism: 'But even then this higher pre-Adamite suppositious Creation must have had an Origin and Creator; for a Creator is a more natural imagination than a fortuitous concourse of atoms. All things remount to a fountain, though they may flow to an Ocean.'[20] Hence the use of Cuvier's theories in Cain is entirely in keeping with Byron's conception of a divine creation. 'Out of chaos God made a world,'[21] and from this belief in a Creator

---

(1812); From the Portugese (1813-15); Farewell! If Ever Fondest Prayer (1814); When Coldness Wraps this Suffering Clay (1815); Childe Harold, iii, st. 108 (1816); Monk of Athos, st. 3 (1816?); Childe Harold, iv, st. 155 (1818). See also Donner, pp. 51-52, and Eimer, p. 58, ibid., 204 ff., Anhang I.

[16]Taine, IV, 36.

[17]See Letters, V, 406, and Kennedy's Conversations, p. 135; cf. Gamba's testimony, quoted by Kennedy, p. 377, and Galt, p. 268.

[18]During school days at Harrow, 'I fought Lord Calthorpe for writing "D----d Atheist!" under my name.'—Medwin, p. 37. See also his letters in defense of Cain, (Chap. II) for the same indignation.

[19]To observe the frequency with which Byron affirmed or implied his belief in a deity, note Letters: I, 259 (1810); II, 221-223 (1813); III, 403 (1813); III, 60 (1814); VI, 261, note 2 (1815-16); Seventeen Letters, p. 41 (1816); V, 15 (1820); V, 132 (1820); see also Medwin, pp. 52-53 (1821-2); Letters, VI, 38-39 (1822); Letters, VI, 182 (1823); Don Juan, xi, st. 6 (1822); Kennedy, p. 46, p. 74, and p. 135 (1823). Cain and Heaven and Earth necessarily reflect a theistic conception.

[20]Letters, V, 459 (1821).

[21]Letters, V, 152 (1821).

Byron never departed.[22]

    Byron's acceptance of the belief in a Creator was by
no means a rationalistic or philosophical theism. It was the
product of religious teaching, grounded upon the Old Testament,[23] and conceived in the spirit of the Psalmist, 'What is
man, that thou art mindful of him?' The insignificance of
man in the face of creation was always present to Byron:

> How beautiful is all this visible world!
> How glorious in its action and itself!
> But we, who name ourselves its sovereigns, we,
> Half dust, half deity, alike unfit
> To sink or soar, with our mix'd essence make
> A conflict of its elements, and breathe
> The breath of degradation and of pride.
> > Manfred, I.ii.297-303 (1816).

It is found in his earliest poetry, and is intimately associated with the development of his 'natural religion' and
his pantheism. It gains steadily in volume until in Cain it
is used as the motivation of the murder of Abel: 'The ob-
ject of the Demon is to depress him still further in his own
estimation than he was before, by showing him the infinite
things and his own abasement, till he falls into the frame of
mind that leads to the Catastrophe, from mere internal irrita-
tion, not premeditation, or envy of Abel (which would have
made him contemptible), but from the rage and fury against
the inadequacy of his state to his conceptions. . . .'[24]

    The state of mind with which Byron approached specula-
tion about the nature of the Deity was hence not logical conviction but religious awe. The Divine nature was to him not
a metaphysical principle but a Being of conscious will and
purpose. Byron has little to say specifically upon this
score, but much that he wrote in the tradition of 'natural
religion' inherited from the eighteenth century, concerned

---

[22]Cf. Prayer of Nature, passim (1806); Adieu, 101 ff. (1807); Letters,
II, 54 ff.: 'Great First Cause' and 'Creator' (1811); Letters, III,
401 ff.: 'I believe doubtless in God. . . .reverence for the Creator'
(1813); Giaour, 1139: 'A Ray of him who form'd the whole' (1813); Childe
Harold, iii, st. 109 (1816); Kennedy, p. 220 (1823). There are of course
many more implicit avowals that he conceived of the Deity as a Creator,
not here cited.

[23]See Letters, V, 391 (1821): 'I am a great reader and admirer of
those books, and had read them through and through before I was eight
years old,—that is to say, the Old Testament, for the New struck me as a
task, but the other a pleasure.' Pönitz, p. 119, confirms the fact that
Byron preferred the Old Testament. Note also Seventeen Letters, p. 39:
'I have begun the Bible (O. T.) again, and shall wade into Job tomorrow,
with whom I feel myself at home: Adios! (1816).

[24]Letters, V, 470. Cf. Prayer of Nature, 53 (1806); Adieu, 109 (1807);

primarily with the teleological argument from design, assumes
the Divine to be a personality, a Being possessed of purpose
and hence of consciousness.[25] Cain and Heaven and Earth show
most markedly Byron's concern with the Divine purpose. Whatever skepticism may be traced in these dramas, there is no
question that Byron assumed the existence of divine will:

> all
> Rests upon thee; and good and evil seem
> To have no power themselves, save in thy will.
>   Cain, III.i.273-275[26]

It was characteristic of Byron that, of the attributes
ascribed to the Deity by traditional theology, he should concern himself in large measure with will and power, that is to
say, with divine sovereignty. The power of the supreme will
to intervene in natural process is a tenet of theism, not of
deism or of pantheism. Byron had moods of skepticism, of
course, in which he denied the possibility of divine intervention.[27] But the letter to Hodgson in which he denies the
possibility of miracles was written only ten days after he
had admitted to the same man his confidence in 'the God who
punishes in this existence.'[28] Byron's Hebraic sense of the

---

Letters, II, 222 (1813); Letters, III, 408 (1814); Manfred, I.ii.297-303
(1816); Childe Harold, iv, st. 32, v. 5 (1818); Vision of Judgment, st.
40 (1821); Letters, VI, 388 (appendix to Foscari, pub. 1821); Cain,
II.ii.625-27; ibid., III.i.67-69; ibid., III.i.113-115; ibid., III.i.179-
83 (1821); Letters, VI, 18, 55-56, 132 (1822); Deformed Transformed,
I.ii.890-897; ibid., III.137-149 (1822); Don Juan, ix, st. 13 (1822);
Blessington, p. 294 (1823). See also Eimer, p. 46 ff.

[25]See below, Chap. III, for Byron's strong interest in and dependence
upon the pietistic poetry of Young, whose naturalism is supplemental to
his theism. See also Prayer of Nature, vv. 31-32, the 'great Creator's
purpose' (1806); cf. Letters, II, 34 ff.: 'I throw myself on the mercy
of the "Great First Cause, least understood," who must do what is most
proper; though I conceive He never made anything to be tortured in another life, whatever it may in this' (1811).

[26]See also Cain, I.1.263-264; ibid., II.ii.247-248 (1821); Heaven and
Earth, I.iii.1125-1128 (1821).

[27]Letters, II, 34 ff.: 'As to miracles, I agree with Hume that it is
more probable men should lie or be deceived, than that things out of the
course of Nature should so happen' (to Hodgson, Sept. 13, 1811). See
also Poetical Works, I, 123, note 1 (1806); Letters, VI, 147 (1822); Letters, VI, 265 (1823); and Don Juan, ix, st. 19 (1822).

[28]Letter to Hodgson, Sept. 3, 1811, Letters, II, 18 ff. See also
Letters, V, 554 (1821) for a momentary acceptance of belief in Christ's
miracles.

insignificance of man in the Creation hence had a counterpart in his perception of the disparity between the human
and the divine will.

> Unequal is the strife
> Between our strength and the Eternal Might!
> Heaven and Earth, I.iii.1038-8 (1821)[29]

It was the emphasis which Augustine, and after him
Calvin, placed upon the sovereignty of God that led them to
elaborate the doctrine of predestination. There is inherent
in Calvinistic theology a determinism which, to a mind im-
perfectly trained in the subtleties of theological argument,
may seem virtually absolute.[30] Hence it was that Byron told
Kennedy: 'On predestination. . . .it appears to me, just
from my own reflections and experiences, that I am influenced
in a way which is incomprehensible, and am led to do things
which I never intended; and if there is, as we all admit, a
Supreme Ruler of the universe, and if, as you say, he has the
actions of the devils, as well as of his own angels, completely at his command, then those influences, or those ar-
rangements of circumstances, which lead us to do things
against our will, or with ill-will, must be also under his
direction. But I have never entered into the depths of the
subject, but contented myself with believing that there is a
predestination of events, and that that predestination de-
pends on the will of God.'[31]
    That Byron, the supreme exponent of will, should be
also a determinist, is of course an apparent paradox. Professor Chew has elaborated the theory that in his emphasis
upon volition Byron reached the heart of the tragic idea:
the overweening assertion of the will brings with it retribu-
tion in the intrinsic consequences of a tragic singleness of
purpose.[32] But since necessitarianism carried to the point

[29]Cf. On the Death of a Young Lady, vv. 17-20 (1802); Prayer of Nature,
vv. 41-52 (1806); Deformed Transformed, I.ii.599-602 (1822).

[30]See James Orr, 'Calvinism,' Enc. of Religion and Ethics, III, 148:
the Calvinistic system, more than the Lutheran, 'comprehensively considered, affirms the entire dependence of all things in nature and grace,
in their being, ordering, and capacity for good, on God.'

[31]Kennedy, p. 189. Cf. ibid., p. 172 (1823); Letters, V, 286 (1821)
for humorous reference; Don Juan, x, st. 54-55 (1822); Letters, VI, 314
(1824); Letters V, 186-7: 'no one can know whether he is sure of salvation. . . .a single slip of faith may throw him on his back, like a
skaiter' (1821); Letters, II, 19 (1807): 'all the virtues and pious Deeds
performed on Earth can never entitle a man to Everlasting happiness in a
future State.'

[32]S. C. Chew, Dramas of Lord Byron, Chapters IV and IX. Du Bos (Byron
and the Need of Fatality) might have illuminated further Byron's

at which it will crush human resistance is incompatible with
tragedy, Professor Chew is inclined to minimize Byron's determinism, and to maintain that (except for Sardanapalus)[33]
the dramas are not fatalistic.

It seems unlikely, however, that Byron ever arrived
at any solution of the old dilemma implied between the doctrines of predestination and free-will; Calvinistic training
was moreover well calculated to withhold him from making of
the logical difficulty involved a principle destructive of
his belief in either foreordination or in freedom of choice.
It is quite true that the imperious will of the Byronic hero
as he appears in the Oriental tales, the sense of moral responsibility in Manfred, or Childe Harold's confession 'I
should have known what fruit would spring from such a seed'
all imply liberty of choice. But it is also true, as Professor Chew himself points out, that Manfred is perfectly
submissive to the power above Arimanes, just as Shelley's
Prometheus accepts without question the rule of Demogorgon,
the fate above Zeus. Even in Lucifer's defiant outburst
against 'the Omnipotent tyrant,' he recognizes that 'I have
a victor.'[34] And it is to be noted that Don Juan's serenity
consists largely in the faculty of keeping his head above
water with the minimum of resistance.[35] Mr. Paul Elmer More
has pointed out that the greatness of Don Juan arises partly
from the spirit of epic fortitude in the face of broken
aspirations and human littleness.[36]

There is nothing more characteristic of Byron than
the trait which the Countess of Blessington called 'a help-
lessness. . . .a sort of abandonment of himself to his
destiny, as he called it.'[37] At the peak of his popularity in

---

determinism had he been more concerned with Byron's thoughts and less with
his amours, and had he not vitiated his study for present purposes by
disavowing any interest in Byron's poetry or liking for it (p. 153).

[33]The determinism of Sardanapalus is correspondence between mundane
happenings and astral influences. Byron introduced the idea of astral
forces frequently; in the early poetry it is largely traditional in de-
rivation: Letters, I, 161 (1808); To a Knot, v. 32 (1806); English
Bards, v. 778 (1809); Childe Harold, i, st. 47 (1812); Letters, III, 152
(1814). See also Manfred I.i.110-131; Lament of Tasso 139 (1817);
Sardanapalus, particularly II.i.66, III.i.275-282 (1821).

[34]Cain, II.ii.634.

[35]See also F. W. Moorman, Cambridge History of English Literature, on
the character of Don Juan.

[36]P. E. More, Shelburne Essays, pp. 171-174.

[37]Blessington, p. 361. Cf. op. cit., pp.271-2: 'We are all the
creatures of circumstance; the greater part of our errors are caused, if
not excused [there speaks the Calvinist], by events and situations over
which we have had little control. . . .' Cf. his own more recently published letter: 'But fate compels me, and necessity, and I can no more

London, before the clouds began to gather, he wrote, 'Who can command circumstances? The most we can do is to avail our-selves of them.'[38] Five years later, surveying the ruin of his life, came the lines:

> And Circumstance, that unspiritual god
> And miscreator, makes and helps along
> Our coming evils with a crutch-like rod,
> Whose touch turns Hope to dust,--the dust we all have trod.
> Childe Harold, iv, st. 125 (1816).

This was the philosophy of Johnson as he stood chained with Juan in the slave market.[39] And it came to Byron's aid when he received the news of Allegra's death: 'But it is a moment when we are apt to think that, if this or that had been done, such event might have been prevented,--though every day and hour shows us that they are the most natural and inevitable. I suppose that Time will do his usual work--Death has done his.'[40]

It will be noted that Byron paid little attention to precise distinctions between doctrines. As he told Kennedy, 'I have never entered into the depths of the subject.' Byron was hence prone to confuse his deterministic philosophy with the purely theological doctrine of predestination. He did not always distinguish between the sovereignty of the divine will and that other aspect of predestination which implies that man, through divine grace, is enabled to win eternal life. For Byron, it was all 'predestination of events.' But the significance of Byron's Calvinistic training was not in the details of what he believed; it was rather in the awed sense of man's relative impotence before the operations of

---

help sinning now than I could save myself from damnation, hereafter.'-- Seventeen Letters, p. 45 (1817).

[38]Correspondence, I, 202 (1813).

[39]
> To strive, too, with our fate were such a strife
> As if the corn-sheaf should oppose the sickle:
> Men are the sport of circumstances, when
> The circumstances seem the sport of men.
> Don Juan, v, st. 17 (1820).

[40]Letters, VI, 54 (1822). Cf. ibid., 50, note 2: 'however deeply human scrutiny may pry into the infinitely perplexed combination of events--how-ever accurately human prudence may understand, arrange, and make use of what it knows--it still ever remains confined, nor even dreams of a thousand matters which come forth from the womb of the next hour.' Cf. Childe Harold, iii, st. 70 (1816); Ode on Venice, 60-65 (1818); Don Juan, i, st. 116 (1818); Sardanapalus, III.i.320 (1821); Letters, V, 451, De-tached Thoughts, No. 85 (1821); Don Juan, vii, st. 76 (1822).

divine law, and the strong infusion of that mood in his
poetry.

That Byron's conception of the Deity was primarily
Hebraic rather than Christian is rendered even more apparent
by his conception of the nature and personality of Christ.
Byron did not show much interest in the New Testament, with
its message of comfort and hope, until late years. He did
not mention Christ in his poetry until he was twenty-three.
One should note that the evidences of Byron's interest in
the Redeemer correspond in their development and nature with
the evidences of his tendency toward the Roman communion.

His very earliest references to Christ are contained
in the rather stilted letters to Hodgson, where, among his
other skeptic tendencies, he denies the justice and the prob-
ability of a vicarious atonement.[41] Byron missed entirely
the significance of the teaching that by union with Christ
there may follow a mystic participation in the crucifixion
and resurrection; he never accepted the atonement as a timeless and universal act of expiation. The Platonic idealism
upon which the doctrine was erected was utterly foreign to
him at that time of his life. He was, in the medieval sense,
a nominalist; the individual existence, and the guilt peculiar
to that existence, were the only realities. And although in
Cain the expression is less crude, the same point of view is
quite apparent:

> Adah. How know we that some such atonement one day
>   May not redeem our race?
> Cain.   By sacrificing
>   The harmless for the guilty? what atonement
>   Were there?
>   Cain, III.1.85-88 (1821).

As for other traditional doctrines about the personality and nature of Christ, his skepticism is largely confined
to his youth, and is closely associated in his mind with a
strong anti-Catholicism which was later to be modified by his
stay in Catholic Italy. The doctrine of the virgin birth is
thus inextricably entangled in his verse with that of the

[41]See Letters, II, 18 ff. (1811): 'As to revealed religion, Christ
came to save men; but a good Pagan will go to heaven, and a bad Nazarene
to hell.' Cf. ibid., 54 ff.: 'The basis of your religion is injustice;
the Son of God, the pure, the immaculate, the innocent, is sacrificed for
the Guilty. This proves His heroism; but no more does away man's guilt
than a schoolboy's volunteering to be flogged for another would exculpate
the dunce. . . . You degrade the Creator. . . .and. . . .you convert Him
into a Tyrant over an immaculate and injured Being, who is sent into
existence to suffer death for the benefit of some millions of Scoundrels.
who, after all, seem as likely to be damned as ever.!

immaculate conception and with the Catholic adoration of the
Virgin.[42]

By 1815, however, Byron shows that tendency toward
Catholicism which seemed to carry.with it an increasing reverence for the person of Christ. First, by implication, and
later, by direct avowal, he accepted the divinity of Christ.[43]
A growing sympathy with the tradition even allowed him to ex-
press, albeit through characters dramatically conceived, a
momentary imaginative acceptance of the vicarious atonement.[44]

This is not to say that Byron was approaching a 'conversion' of any kind. His skeptical tendencies precluded
that. The significance of Byron's interest in the personality
of Christ is the lateness of its development. Not until maturity did he come to a sympathetic attitude toward the Christian system of grace. The relation of the creature to the
Creator, or, in traditional language, the salvation of man,
appeared to him during his formative years in its Hebraic
rather than in its Christian aspect; his early poetry ignores
the New Testament teaching of a divine mediator between man
and God. Although he came finally to conceive of Christ as a
divine teacher,[45] he seldom concerned himself with Christ as
a redeemer. The later speculative poems, Cain and Heaven and
Earth, are hence conceived in the spirit of the Old Testament.
The wrath of Jehovah is to be averted by submission, not by
faith in a redeemer.

Again, Byron's tendency to treat of the divine as a
Person rather than as a principle is Hebraic rather than
Christian in deriving the personal nature of the Deity from

[42]To be taken up in greater detail in Chapter IV. Cf. Correspondence,
I, 122 (1812) and Childe Harold, ii, st. 44 (1812). The references to
Christ and the Virgin in the note to The Waltz, v. 21, (1812), although
extremely coarse, are not aimed at the personality of Christ. A recurrence
of the same mood, surprisingly late, is found in Don Juan, xi, st. 6 (1822).

[43]He had never really denied the supernatural element in Christ, except
that in rejecting the virgin birth he had rejected one of the traditional
'evidences.' See Siege of Corinth, vv. 955 and 1003 (1815); Childe Harold,
iii, st. 9, v. 3 and note thereto (1816); Letters, V, 554 (1821); Don
Juan, xv, st. 18 and note thereto (1816); Letters, V, 554 (1821); Don
Juan, xv, st. 18 and note thereto (1823); Don Juan, iii, st. 103 (the
famous 'Ave Maria' passage, 1819).

[44]Note that even in the letters to Hodgson, he had seemed to connect
Christ with the salvation of men. See particularly Prophecy of Dante,
iii, v. 122 (1819); Deformed Transformed, I.ii.611 (1822); and Heaven and
Earth, I.iit.471-472 (1821).

[45]See Letters, III, 401 ff. (1813): '. . . .the moral of Christianity
is perfectly beautiful. . . .'; Letters, V, 554 (1821): 'What proved
Jesus Christ the Son of God hardly less than his miracles? His moral pre-
cepts.'

the Hebrew belief in a self-conscious Unitary Creator possessed of sovereign will, rather than from the Christian
teaching of a Trinity of persons. Here again, Byron's individualism, or, in the medieval sense, his nominalism, refused to accept the fundamentally Greek idea of universale
ante rem. Even when, in later years, he confessed that 'if
ever God was man--or man God--he [Christ] was both,'[46] he
still found the doctrines of a triune God 'quite appalling,'[47]
or as 'mystical' as Plato's teaching.[48]

A direct consequence of Byron's conception of the
Deity was his sense of a vast gulf between God and the world.
He believed in a type of dualism found in most theistic systems. It is characteristic of Deism to imply such a gulf,
since Deism conceives of the First Cause as existing apart
from the Creation and its processes. But Byron's sense of
lowliness did not originate in a philosophical conviction of
the transcendence of God.[49] It should be interpreted as a
reflection of his close attention to the Judaistic element in
Christianity and of the relatively minor emphasis he placed
upon the mediation of a divine Person between man and God. It
is essentially akin to his sense of insignificance before the
vastness of the visible creation, and to his feeling of impotence in a fatalistic universe.

A distinction should be made between the early poetry,
with its traditional expressions of the insignificance of man,
and the more mature expressions of his later years.[50]

[46]Note to Don Juan, XV, st. 18 (1823).

[47]Kennedy, p. 176. Cf. ibid., p. 182 (1823).

[48]Medwin, p. 51: 'You believe in Plato's three principles; why not in
the Trinity?' he asked Shelley. 'One is not more mystical than the other'
(1821-2). For other remarks on the Trinity see Devil's Drive, vv. 237-248
(1813); Don Juan, xi, st. 6 (1822). Note also Prophecy of Dante, i, vv.
13-15 (1819), influenced by Paradiso, xxxiii, 115-120, as an example of
Byron's imaginative sympathy with a character dramatically conceived.

[49]Donner and Eimer both reached the conclusion that Byron was a Deist.
It is perfectly true that his skeptical tendencies were similar to those
associated in eighteenth century thought with Deism. As a young man he
once called himself a Deist (Letters, II, 19, to Ensign Long, 1807). But
Byron's Calvinistic background and his life-long preoccupation with theological dogma led to a state of mind seldom associated with Deism. His
moods of agitated denial and brooding depression were utterly unlike the
easy assurance of Voltaire and the English rationalists.

[50]See particularly Prayer of Nature, V, 31: 'reptiles, grovelling on
the ground' (1806); Adieu, v. 109: 'a child of dust' (1807); A Spirit
Pass'd Before Me: 'Things of a day! you wither ere the night' (1814);
Childe Harold, iv, st. 155 (1818):

Particularly during 1821, when he was occupied with the Biblical dramas, this sense of awe was constantly present in his
mind. Cain and Heaven and Earth are conceived entirely in
this spirit. He is concerned in these dramas not only to show
the insignificance of man, but to portray the separation of
man and God from each other.[51] It was his deliberate intention
to do so; and his own belief that such a representation was
not alien to the spirit of traditional religion forms a part
of his defense of Cain: 'I have even avoided introducing the
Deity, as in Scripture. . . .on purpose to avoid shocking any
feelings on the subject by falling short of what all unin-
spired men must fall short in, viz., giving an adequate notion of the effect of the presence of Jehovah.' [52] It was not
merely to avoid giving offense that Byron excluded the Deity
from his dramatis personae. He had a personal aversion to
'too great a familiarity with Heaven,' as his criticism of
Milton several times implies. [53] He attacked Southey on the
same grounds, and in the Vision of Judgment, the better to re-
buke Southey, he carefully avoided making the Deity talk 'like
a school divine.'[54]

> . . . .and thou
> Shalt one day, if found worthy, so defined,
> See thy God face to face as thou dost now
> His Holy of Holies, nor be blasted by his brow.

[51]Cf. Cain, I.i.147-151:

> But let him
> Sit on his vast and solitary throne,
> Creating worlds, to make eternity
> Less burthensome to his immense existence
> And unparticipated solitude;
> Let him crowd orb on orb: he is alone. . . .

See also Heaven and Earth, I.iii.740-742, 957-960, 635-640:

> Unions like to these,
> Between a mortal and an immortal, cannot
> Be happy or be hallow'd. We are sent
> Upon the earth to toil and die; and they
> Are made to minister on high unto
> The Highest.

[52]Letters, VI, 15 ff. (1822).
[53]See Medwin, p. 47 (1821-2). Cf. his criticism of Townsend for 'tell-
ing the Lord what he is to do, Letters, II, 9 (1811); his statement that
Milton is 'absurd (and, in fact, blasphemous) in putting material light-
nings into the hands of the Godhead,' Letters, V, 555 (1821); cf. Letters,
VI, 15 ff. (1822) for similar reference to Milton.
[54]Postscript to Preface of Vision of Judgment (1821). Cf. his characterization of Southey as 'ludicrous and blasphemous' in 'Note to Appendix' of Two Foscari, Letters, VI, 589 (pub. 1821).

The spectacle of Byron lecturing Southey on his want
of reverence must have seemed strange to Byron's contemporaries, many of whom were thoroughly convinced that his lordship was the most thorough-going infidel in Europe. But one
can hardly escape the conclusion that Byron's mind was fundamentally religious--religious, not in the sense of orthodox
piety, but in the sense of a being innately predisposed to
concern itself with the supernatural order, or to inquire
into the bearing of traditional beliefs upon human experience.
     To a mind of that stamp, sin and its consequences are
of prime importance. Byron's awe in the presence of all that
lies beyond ordinary experience, and his exaggerated sense of
guilt, are closely connected with the strong emphasis placed
upon the doctrine of original sin by Calvinistic creeds. It
would be hard to find a mentality more likely than his to be
thrown into a state of emotional agitation by such a doctrine.
His blazing sense of justice, his passionate desire for a
state in which the guiltless should be unmolested and the
wicked should be restrained, made Byron preëminently the poet
of revolution. Yet he was confronted with a dogma which laid
upon him and all men the guilt for another's misdeed. The
medieval realism of Augustine, which considered Adam as an
archetype in whose essential being all other men necessarily
participated, meant nothing to Byron with his passionate
realization of individual existence. His concrete egoism,
translated into the haughty defiance of Manfred and the trucu-
lent mutterings of Cain, was by its very essence alien to all
concepts which would render doubtful the reality of the Ego,
or which would merge its existence, its griefs and joys, in a
timeless, archetypal substance:

          The mind which is immortal makes itself
          Requital for its good or evil thoughts,
          Is its own origin of ill and end,
          And its own time and place.
               Manfred, III.iv.389-392 (1817).

     How else could this poet of self, of revolution, of
defiance, view a creed which taught him that for another's
fault he was obnoxious in the sight of his Creator? How
should he answer those who

          Tell us that all, for one who fell,
               Must perish in the mingling storm?
               Prayer of Nature, 23-24 (1806).

     Yet he could not ignore a doctrine which, however un-
intelligible, seemed so abundantly proved by the facts of experience. Byron's characteristic misanthropy was entirely in
accord with the theological doctrine of original sin, and

man's resultant depravity. Everything seemed to combine in a
convincing proof--the vicious moral tone of London under the
regency, the animalism of that 'sea-Sodom,' Venice, the de-
fection from the cause of liberty by poets who 'crooked the
pregnant hinges of the knee where thrift might follow fawn-
ing.' Even the low estimate of man in the affected first
cantos of Childe Harold, although in part the superficial
pose of the young roué, is not without significance as the
initial stage of Byron's awareness of the evil in men. In
the young moralist of The Curse of Minerva and The Waltz was
born the master ironist of Beppo and The Vision of Judgment.[55]

Not only in the utter worthlessness of 'that bitter
draught, the human species'[56] does the curse of Jehovah show
its power. The sense of a world accursed becomes a central
theme in the poetry of Weltschmerz:

> Our life is a false nature, 't is not in
> The harmony of things,--this hard decree,
> This uneradicable taint of sin,
> This boundless upas, this all-blasting tree
> Whose root is earth, whose leaves and branches be
> The skies which rain their plagues on men like dew--
> Disease, death, bondage--all the woes we see--
> And worse, the woes we see not--which throb through
> The immedicable soul, with heart-aches ever new.
>   Childe Harold, iv, st. 126 (1818).

''T is not in the harmony of things,' but it is a
fact because 'disease, death, bondage' are facts. They are
but the operations of a retributive principle[57] which first
brought death into the world and all our woe. 'The thought of
a world steeped in sorrow to the lips'[58] is with Byron all
through the composition of the Biblical dramas:

---

[55]It should be noted that Byron endorsed heartily the theological doctrine of total depravity in his conversations with Kennedy, q. v., p. 172:
'I already believe in predestination, which I know you believe, and in the
depravity of the human heart in general, and of my own in particular. . . .'
Cf. op. cit., pp. 139-40, 148, 166-67 (1823). See also Blessington,
p. 310: 'We have a strong and decided predisposition to evil' (1823). His
references to the Fall of Man are very frequent in the later years: Don
Juan, i, st. 127 (1818); ibid., ii, st. 193 (1818-19); ibid., v, st. 49 and
109 (1820); Vision of Judgment, st. 66 (1821); Medwin, p. 149 (1821-22);
Don Juan, ix, st. 19 (1822); ibid., xiv, st. 23 (1823); ibid., xiv, st. 78.
This list does not include the Biblical dramas.

[56]Don Juan, x, st. 73 (1822).

[57]
          And thou, who never yet of human wrong
          Left the unbalanced scale, great Nemesis!
                    Childe Harold, iv, st. 132 (1818).

[58]Stopford Brooke, 'Byron's Cain,' Hibbert Journal, XVIII (1919), 74-94.

The agony to which they must be heirs--
Born to be plough'd with years, and sown with cares,
And reap'd by Death, lord of the human soil.
Even had their days been left to toil their path
Through time to dust, unshorten'd by God's wrath,
Still they are Evil's prey and Sorrow's spoil.
                    Heaven and Earth, I.iii.870-875 (1821).

It was this poignant sense of human suffering, a sense
which no misanthropy could dull, which won for Byron much of
his fame on the continent. 'We discovered it,' says Mazzini,
'we Continentalists; not his own countrymen.'[59] Hence the
Italian liberal was among the first to point out the bitterness of Byron's burlesque--'always suffering--often most so
when he seemed to laugh.' That is the spirit of Don Juan:

So now all things are d--n'd one feels at ease,
    As after reading Athanasius' curse,
Which doth your true believer so much please:
    I doubt if any now could make it worse
O'er his worst enemy when at his knees,
    'T is so sententious, positive, and terse,
And decorates the book of Common Prayer,
As doth a rainbow the just clearing air.
                    Don Juan, vi, st. 23 (1822).

To pass from the general to the particular, Byron was
thoroughly convinced that there lay upon the Byron family a
curse which predestined its members to the expiation of ancestral faults. He knew well enough that to have the blood of
the wicked Byrons in one's veins was no matter for rejoicing.[60]
'It is fit that I should pay the forfeit of my forefathers'
extravagances and my own; and, whatever my faults may be, I
suppose they will be pretty well expiated in time--or eternity.'[61] Hence his readiness to attribute the ills which beset

This is the best discussion of the relation of Byron's Cain to his Calvinistic training that has ever appeared; it treats the subject so ade-
quately that no detailed discussion of Cain is necessary here.

[59]Life and Writings, VI, 70. Cf. Brandes Main Currents, Chap. XX:
'The mark of Cain is the mark of humanity.'

[60]'My sister writes me melancholy letters; things are not going on
well there, but mismanagement is the hereditary epidemic of our brood.'—
Correspondence, I, 46 (1811). Cf. Newstead Abbey (1811):

            And vain was the hope to avert our decline,
            And the fate of my fathers had faded to mine.

[61]Letters, III, 271 (1816); cf. his description of an Alpine landscape:
'Passed whole woods of withered pines. . . .their appearance reminded me
of me and of my family.'—Letters, III, 360 (1816).

him to the Nemesis which pursued the Byrons.

> It is not that I may not have incurr'd
> For my ancestral faults or mine the wound
> I bleed withal, and, had it been conferr'd
> With a just weapon, it had flow'd unbound.
> > Childe Harold, iv, st. 133 (1818).

The strange fatality which seemed to hang over his existence
has been remarked by almost every biographer. Byron thought
he could trace the hand of destiny in the most ordinary circumstances of his kin.[62]   It was a line accursed, for whom
naught but misfortune was to be expected.[63]

His own personal sense of moral guilt was hence rendered morbidly alert. The perversity with which he paraded
his own escapades was in part but a flippant substitution of
bravado for uneasiness; Moore called it 'inverse hypocrisy.'
The traditional expressions of sinfulness,[64] and the exaggerated affectations of viciousness in the first cantos of
Childe Harold may in part be discounted as mere evidences of
immaturity.[65] But there persists in his mind a prepossession
with the mental states associated with guilt indicative of an
acute sensitivity in such matters.[66] Even in the intrigues to

---

[62]'It is very odd that my mother was an only child;—I am an only
child; my wife is an only child; and Ada is an only child. . . .I can't
help thinking it was destined to be so.'—Medwin, p. 65 (1821-2); cf.
Letters, V, 467 (1821).

[63]For his interest in hereditary evil, see the persistence of Cain's
turbulent blood in the character of Aholibamah:

> Too much of the forefather whom thou vauntest
> Has come down in that haughty blood.
> > Heaven and Earth, I.iii.663-664 (1821).

See also the operations of a curse in Werner, V.ii.554-556 (1822):

> Now open wide, my sire, thy grave;
> Thy curse hath dug it deeper for thy son
> In mine! The race of Siegendorf is past!

[64]Prayer of Nature, vv. 3, 6, 8, 39 (1806).

[65]See also Letters, I, 272-3: 'I am tolerably sick of vice, which I
have tried in its agreeable varieties' (1810); Letters, I, 285: 'I have
been guilty of many excesses' (1810); Letters, I, 306: 'my various hopes
in this world almost extinct, and not very brilliant in the next, I trust
I shall go through the process with a creditable sang froid and not dis-
grace a line of cut-throat ancestors' (1810).

[66]See the familiar lines of Giaour, vv. 261-276 (1813); Corsair, x,
227-248 (1813); Manfred, I.ii.288-291 (1816), II.i.69 (1816), III.i.70-78
(1817).

which he devoted so much of his energy he seems never to have
lost his awareness of guilt.[67]

In one of the letters to Lady Melbourne about his relations with 'X,' that is, Augusta Leigh, he writes, 'as for
me, brought up as I was, and sent into the world as I was,
both physically and morally, nothing better could be expected,
and it is odd that I always had a foreboding. . . .'[68] Byron
seems very definitely to have associated his rearing, his
lameness, and his violent blood as integral parts of the
fatality which appeared to rule his life. 'My poor mother was
generally in a rage every day, and used to render me sometimes
almost frantic; particularly when, in her passion, she re-
proached me with my personal deformity; I have left her presence to rush into solitude, where, unseen, I could vent the
rage and mortification I endured, and curse the deformity that
I now began to consider as a signal mark of the injustice of
Providence.'[69] The malformed limb was hence the operation of
an 'unresting doom,'[70] for which he might thank 'my bitch of
a star.'[71] Not shap'd for sportive tricks, made only for his
own misery,[72] he felt always the shadow of an untoward fate in
all that he experienced.

With regard to Byron's lameness, the testimony of Lady
Byron about the effect of Calvinistic training is of great importance. 'To that unhappy view of the relation of the creature to the Creator, I have always ascribed the misery of his
life. . . .It is enough for me to remember, that he who thinks
his transgressions beyond forgiveness (and such was his own

[67]Hence Maurois: 'To the Bible-bred young Scot in Byron, Lady Caroline
was the woman taken in adultery.'—(Byron, p. 191.) His letters to Lady
Melbourne about the intended seduction of Lady Francis Webster are frankly
uneasy about 'the tremendous "beam in my own eye"'; and the 'strongest
mixture of right and wrong' in the lady's justification of her conduct
(Correspondence, I, 184 and I, 216, 1813). Caroline Lamb's folly he flip-
pantly traces to 'original sin' (ibid., 109, 1812). See also his admis-
sion to Blessington that 'religion and morals,' although ignored by the
principals of an irregular connection, increase 'tenfold' the 'misery'
which follows it (Conversations, p. 125, 1823).

[68]Correspondence, I, 257 (1814).

[69]Blessington, pp. 111-112; cf. ibid., 328: 'Nature, he said, had to
answer for malignité as well as for deformity; she gave both, and the unfortunate persons on whom she bestowed them were not to be blamed for
their effects' (1823).

[70]   Childe Harold, i, st. 83 (1812):
                    . . . .life-abhorring gloom
        Wrote on his faded brow curst Cain's unresting doom.

[71]Letters, III, 152 (1814).

[72]'. . . .by that God who made me for my own misery, and not much for
the good of others. . . .'—Correspondence, I, 254 (1814).

deepest feeling), has righteousness beyond that of the self-satisfied sinner; or, perhaps, of the half-awakened. It was impossible for me to doubt that, could he have been at once assured of pardon, his living faith in a moral duty and love of virtue ("I love the virtues which I cannot claim") would have conquered every temptation. Judge, then, how I must hate the Creed which made him see God as an Avenger, not a Father. My own impressions were just the reverse, but could have little weight, and it was in vain to seek to turn his thoughts for long from that idée fixe, with which he connect- ed his physical peculiarity as a stamp. Instead of being made happier by any apparent good, he felt that every bless- ing would be "turned into curse" to him. . . . "The worst of it is, I do believe," he said. I, like all connected with him, was broken against the rock of Predestination. I may be pardoned for referring to his frequent expression of the sentiment that I was only sent to show him the happiness he was forbidden to enjoy. You will now better understand why "The Deformed Transformed" is too painful to me for discus- sion.[173]

From all Byron's associates comes the evidence that he was in certain recurrent moods the prey of fears for which nothing external to his native temperament will account save his preoccupation with the most extreme dogmas of Calvinism.[74] His intermittent periods of skepticism were but an added source of agitation.[75] The state of Byron's mind was de- scribed by Shelley in a letter to Horace Smith most vividly-- far more vividly than in the rather incomplete but better known Julian and Maddalo. Shelley wrote, 'Moore. . . .seems to deprecate MY influence on his mind, on the subject of re- ligion, and to attribute the tone assumed in "Cain" to my suggestions. . . . Pray assure him that I have not the

---

[73]Letters, VI, 261, note 2.

[74]Pietro Gamba declared that 'his mind was involved in doubts, which, however, he had a desire to dissipate as troublesome, and on this ac- count he never shunned conversations on this subject, as you well know.'-- Letter to Dr. Kennedy, May 21, 1824, reprinted by Kennedy, p. 375 ff. Medwin, p. 50, also reports Byron to have said to Shelley, 'Here is a little book somebody has sent me about Christianity, that has made me very uncomfortable; the reasoning seems to me very strong, the proofs are very staggering. I don't think you can answer it, Shelley; at least I am sure I can't, and what is more, I don't wish it.' (Underlining my own.)

[75]'I do not know what to believe, or what to disbelieve,' he wrote Hobhouse, 'which is the devil; to have no religion at all! all sense, and senses, are against it; but all belief and much evidence is for it; it is walking in the dark over a rabbit warren, or a garden with steel traps and spring guns.'--Correspondence, II, 46 (1817).

smallest influence over Lord Byron, in this particular, and if
I had, I certainly should employ it to eradicate from his
great mind the delusions of Christianity, which, in spite of
his reason, seem perpetually to recur, and to lay [sic] in
ambush for the hours of sickness and distress.[76]
    Shelley's testimony coincides closely with that of
Byron's other intimate associates and with the evidence found
in his writing and conversation. Byron was haunted by his religious heritage. Although he revolted against it, he could
no more evade the spell it exercised upon him than Hawthorne
could evade the accusing 'gray shadows' of Puritan forefathers who peopled his uneasy fancy. Hawthorne stands in
the same relation to Emerson as Byron does to Shelley.[77]
    A sternly religious background is the only common
denominator for many aspects of Byron's poetry. His over-
powering sense of guilt, deeply infused into the characterization of the Byronic hero, is a direct result of Calvinistic
training. In similar fashion one can trace in Byron's mis-
anthropic tirades the initial impetus of the theological doctrine of total depravity. He rejects the positive or redemp-
tive elements of Christianity for a special aspect of its
tradition, the Hebraic emphasis on the need of submission and
the insignificance of man.
    Certain ideas allied primarily to Protestantism are
constantly present in his thought. He rejected almost entirely the sacramental system, not only because he found its principles difficult of belief, but because his passionate temperament was impatient of aught but immediate contact with that
which absorbed his thoughts. The extreme form of this tendency, the rejection of all that is connected with cult or ecclesiastical organization, was one aspect of his skepticism.
Byron himself would establish his relations with God; there
must be no intervention of priest or ritual. His individualism is essentially Protestant; he is the descendant of the
English nominalists who broke ground for the separatist tendencies of the Reformed faiths. Once, for a brief period, he
felt in Shelley's stimulating presence the identity of all
forms of existence. But the fundamental habit of his thought
was individualistic.

[76]Shelley, Letters, II, 959 (April 11, 1922).
[77]See particularly Hawthorne's introductory chapter to The Scarlet
Letter: 'I know not whether these ancestors of mine bethought themselves
to repent, and ask pardon of Heaven for their cruelties; or whether they
are now groaning under the heavy consequences of them, in another state
of being. At all events, I, the present writer, as their representative,
hereby take shame upon myself for their sakes, and pray that any curse in-
curred by them—as I have heard, and as the dreary and unprosperous con-
dition of the race, for many a long year back, would argue to exist—may
now and henceforth be removed.'

He was therefore totally at variance with that vaguely defined type of thought which for want of a better term we call Platonic.[78] His vision was focussed on the immediate, the singular, the personal. His concern was for the individual human spirit at odds with itself and with other individuals. He could not possibly have been other than a poet of isolation and loneliness.

Eastward from Eden will we take our way;
'T is the most desolate, and suits my steps.

[78]The term is used here in the sense of an habitual tendency to be concerned with the universal and impersonal; it is the type of thought defined in J. A. Stewart's 'Platonism in English Poetry' (English Literature and the Classics, Oxford, 1912).

Chapter Two

S K E P T I C I S M

> For me, I know naught; nothing I deny,
>   Admit, reject, contemn; and what know you?
>   Don Juan, xiv, st. 3.

Pietro Gamba once engaged Byron in a religious discussion, in which the Italian assumed the role of skeptic. 'He answered me with strong arguments and profound eloquence,' wrote Gamba afterward; 'and I perceived that obstinate contradiction on this subject, forcing him to reason upon it, gave him pain.'[1] Gamba had perceived the distress with which Byron always engaged in religious controversy. His vacillation between the acceptance and rejection of traditional doctrines cost a bitter inner struggle of doubt with belief, which is utterly absent from the poetry of Shelley or Wordsworth.

Shelley was not indifferent to traditional beliefs, as his notes to Queen Mab attest, but his repudiation of orthodoxy occasioned no internal conflict. He was serenely confident of his own gospel. And as he matured, his exaltation of love and its power to relieve human suffering carried him closer to the central position of the New Testament. Prometheus Unbound, although hostile to historic dogma, is essentially sympathetic to the Christian concept of a godlike nature inspired by love, securing by its heroic suffering the redemption and liberation of the world.[2] But Shelley reached his ultimate position independently of Christian teaching. Although his thought tended to converge with Christianity in affirming the power of love to elevate mankind, that convergence was fortuitous; it had no bearing on any personal problem occasioned by want of conviction.

---

[1] Letter to Kennedy May 21, 1824. Reprinted by Kennedy, p. 575 ff.

[2] Hence Browning: 'Had Shelley lived he would have finally ranged himself with the Christians.'--Essay on Shelley. His most sympathetic recognition of the character of Christ is evidenced in the Prologue to Hellas. Note also the chorus beginning:

> A Power from the unknown God,
>   A Promethean Conqueror came;
> Like a triumphal path he trod
>   The thorns of death and shame.
>   --Hellas

The story of Wordsworth's changing relation to Christianity is sharply distinguished from that of Byron by the fact that Wordsworth's later preoccupation with orthodox doctrines is not, like Byron's constant recurrence to them, the evidence of inability to reconcile them with his own ideas, but rather of the growing satisfaction he found in them. The passing of the revolutionary Wordsworth was marked by an alteration in 'his attitude toward those institutions, practices, and modes of expression, by which religious feeling is outwardly manifested. . . .he began to respect and appreciate, and later he learned to love, the specific means by which Christendom has attained and embodied human conceptions.'[3] Wordsworth effected this widening of his horizon the more readily because he had never issued an active challenge to the fundamental doctrines of Christianity. What inward struggle there may have been is not reflected, as in Byron, by a continual return to the problems of sin and guilt as they are treated by traditional authority.

Byron is unlike either of his great contemporaries in his inability to arrive either at firm belief or at utter rejection of the doctrines of Christianity. It remained for him a personal difficulty of consummate importance. He is the poet of self; hence his poetry, habitually concerned with his own experience, is replete with discussion of religious beliefs. His letters amply demonstrate that at all times he was given to reflection about the significance of his personal experience, and its relation to traditional beliefs in which he might discover an explanation of his problems. He never found any system of thought which wholly answered this need. Belief was always interrupted by doubt, and in his swift changes of mood there arose a controversial attitude toward traditional belief which constitutes an essential part of his poetry. To understand Byron it is necessary to examine the nature and grounds of his constantly recurring doubts. They represent an inward struggle so intense that he was forced to give poetic expression to the experience.[4]

'The same prematurity of development which brought his passions and genius so early into action,' says Thomas Moore in his treatment of Byron's skepticism, 'enabled him also to anticipate this worst, dreariest result of reason; and at the very time of life when a spirit and temperament like his most required control, those checks, which religious prepossessions

[3]G. M. Harper, William Wordsworth, New York, 1929, Chapter XX, 'Crisis of Middle Life.' Cf. ibid: " He did not 'go over' to popular Christianity. He learned to include it in the great circle of his sympathy."

[4]Guiccioli describes his state of mind as 'une espèce de doute expectant, un ètat de l'esprit qui désire et qui attend une démonstration décisive, pour repousser l'erreur et saluer la vérité.'—Tome I, p. 235.

best supply, were almost wholly wanting.'[5] Thus, between
Byron's lapses from English standards of morality and his
avowed skepticism, even an intimate friend of Byron's saw a
relationship at once unfortunate and reprehensible. Moore
tried to defend Byron wherever possible, but there could be
no weaker defense than the tone of apologetic regret which
Moore adopted. As a man of the world, Moore knew that if
there was anything which British orthodoxy would not tolerate,
it was the avowal of irreligion. Kennedy, Moore, and Guiccioli all treat Byron's skepticism as an inexplicable perver-
sion. Moore suggests that his friend's religious doubts were
caused by Byron's friendship with Charles Skinner Matthews,[6]
but he offers the story of their friendship, not so much in
explanation of Byron's heresies as in extenuation of them.

It is quite obvious that no single influence upon the
mental development of Byron will suffice to explain his departures from orthodox thought. He was not merely aping
Charles Skinner Matthews, nor was he idly amusing himself by
shocking the smug and the conservative elements in British
society. His skepticism resulted from the inborn need for a
vigorous mind to exert itself regardless of the nature of its
conclusions, and from the catholicity of his experience among
both books and men.

Byron himself explains his hostility to established
forms of belief by the fact that his earliest recollections
of religious observances were associated with the memory of
harsh treatment received from his elders.[7] But it is extremely unlikely that the unhappiness of his childhood years
would predispose him to rationalistic thought; it accounts
neither for the force nor for the direction of Byron's heretical bent. It provides only sufficient ground for one to conclude that from early years he was likely to be attracted to
any ideas which appeared to weaken the authority of those
teachings which caused him distress but which he could neither
forget nor fully reject.

Manfred Eimer has shown conclusively that Byron's intellectual development was strongly influenced by his interest
in the conclusions of natural science.[8] Geology, astronomy,
and palaeontology exercised a steadily increasing influence
upon his mind. It was a day in which developmental theories
of the world were sharply challenging the absolutism based on
divine revelation. Moreover, in so far as it is characteristic of naturalistic thought to establish its methods and results on those of physical science, and to ignore everything
spiritual and transcendental, an eager attention to natural

[5]Thomas Moore, Life and Letters of Byron, Chap. VI.
[6]Loc. cit.
[7]See Letters, II, 222 (1813); cf. op. cit., III, 401 ff. (1813).
[8]See below, Chap. III.

science may easily associate itself with skepticism of traditional religious thought. But Eimer finds no certain evidence
of the profound effect of scientific interests upon Byron's
poetry until 1814.[9] This is not early enough to account for
the initial evidences of Byron's skepticism. In the Prayer of
Nature and in the early correspondence the marks of heretical
thought are already plainly in evidence.[10]

Eimer also analyzes Byron's extensive indebtedness to
the literature of the eighteenth century, and explains his
truculence toward the authoritative tradition by the influence
of champions of 'natural religion' in the preceding century.[11]
But he has not fully recognized that in the literature of the
Augustan era Byron discovered a purely rationalistic basis for
skepticism. Neither the poetry of natural religion, nor the
study of natural sciences, are by themselves sufficient to explain his hostility to dogma. It was the cosmopolitan toler-
ance of the literature of the eighteenth century contrasted
with the exclusiveness of earlier Christianity that first led
Byron to abjure the Calvinism which he could not erase from
memory, though he would fain have done so.

From the earliest days of the Reformation English
thought has cherished in one form or another the right to dissent. This was its characteristic in the seventeenth century.[12] Opposition to exclusiveness in religion comes down
through the literature of the next century in a form readily
accessible to the young Byron. The timelessness and ubiquity
of religious truth are constantly affirmed by the Deist, by
the exponent of 'natural religion,' and by poets not primarily occupied with religious discussion.

As a champion of eighteenth-century poetry Byron
could scarcely avoid the influence of that literature in
which cosmopolitanism becomes critical of an intolerant
orthodoxy. It is found in Pope, Byron's earliest master.[13]
Byron claimed in 1807 to have read Gibbon's History, where he
found 'the philosophic and pleasing idea, that notwithstanding
the variety of names, of rites, and of opinions, all the sects

[9]Eimer, pp. 46-49.

[10]See Letters, II, 18 ff. (1807, 1811); ibid., 34 ff. (1811); ibid.,
48 (1811); Correspondence, I, 122 (1812); and particularly Childe Harold,
ii, st. 1-7 and 44 (1812).

[11]See Schmidt, Rousseau and Byron, p. 87 ff.

[12]See Milton's philosophical justification of dissent in Areopagitica:
"There be who perpetually complain of schisms and sects, and make it such
a calamity that any man dissents from their maxims. . . .To be still
searching what we know not by what we know, still closing up truth to
truth, as we find it. . . .this is the golden rule in theology. . . ."

[13]See Weiser, pp.13-14, for similarities between Pope's Universal
Prayer and Byron's Prayer of Nature (1806). Richter concurs, p. 74.

and all the nations of mankind are united in the worship of
the Common Father and Creator of the universe.'[14] All through
Byron's early manhood are to be traced the evidences of his
interest in earlier cosmopolitans. Lady Mary Wortley Montagu
won his especial approbation.[15] The device of a foreign observer to suggest the relativity of cultural values and to
criticize one culture by the standards of another he had already observed by 1810 in Goldsmith's Traveller. The next
year he had read Fougeret de Monbron's Le Cosmopolite, ou le
Citoyen du Monde.[16] The cosmopolitan motif appears so frequently in the works of writers earlier than Byron that he
can scarcely be said to have followed the suggestion of an individual source; he simply adopted a literary fashion which
had long been current.

The directions which such a theory of religious criticism may suggest are many. What shall become of the millions
who by the accident of birth have no knowledge of the Christian religion? 'Some millions must be wrong, that's pretty
clear.'[17] And yet peoples deprived of the regulative bene-
fits of Christianity maintain cultures which compare quite
favorably with that of the Christian nations. 'Their religion makes little difference in their manner of conduct.' 'I
will bring you ten Mussulmans shall shame you in all goodwill
towards men, prayer to God, and duty to their neighbors.' The
Moslem, as a matter of fact, is more minutely faithful to his
creed than the Christian.[18] Even the excesses of rigor which
he displays in the treatment of subject Christians are no
worse than the British policy in Ireland.[19] Nor are these
the observations of a provincial, but those of a man who

[14]Gibbon, Decline and Fall, Chap. XX. See Moore, Chapter V, for Byron's
list of books he had read by 1807, where Gibbon is named. The familiar
stanza of Childe Harold, iii, st. 107, is evidence that Byron had not overlooked Gibbon's treatment of Christianity.

[15]He mentions her first in 1810 (Letters, I, 280). See Index, Letters,
VI, 567, for his numerous references to her. Lady Mary was convinced that
one religion was quite as good as another. See her Letters (New York,
1914): to Lady Rich, Sept. 20, 1716; to Abbé Conti, April 1, 1717 and
May 29, 1717.

[16]For reference to Goldsmith, see Letters, I, 268 (1810); Monbron is
quoted Letters, II, 39 (1811), and several sentences from the same source
are quoted at the head of the Preface of Childe Harold i. He had also
found the foreign observer used in Candide (Letters, II, 36, 1811) and in
Rasselas (Poetical Works, III, 144, note 1).

[17]Don Juan, xv, st. 90; cf. Letters, II, 18 ff. (1811): 'Who will be-
lieve that God will damn men for not knowing what they were never taught?'
Cf. Letters, II, 34 ff. (1811): 'I trust that God is not a Jew, but the
God of all Mankind.' Cf. Medwin, p. 48.

[18]Letters, I, 254 (1809); op. cit., II, 18 ff. (1811); op. cit., III,
402 (1813).

[19]Note to Childe Harold, ii (1812), Poetical Works, II, 206-7.

boasts himself to have seen 'almost every persuasion under the
sun; including most of our own sectaries, and the Greek, the
Catholic, the Armenian, the Lutheran, the Jewish, and the
Mahometan.'[20]
     Criticism of this kind implicitly denies the validity
of the 'seventy-two villainous sects who are tearing each
other to pieces for the love of the Lord and hatred of each
other.'[21]   The mutual inconsistency of dogmatic systems of
thought is an index of their unreliability.[22] Persecution
and intolerance can therefore not be justified; the true cos-
mospolite is unalterably opposed to absolutism in religious
or philosophical thought.
     The forms which Byron's skepticism was likely to take
in his earlier poetry are hence as diverse as the causes of
his unorthodoxy. A personally repellent content in historic
Christianity as it was first presented to Byron excited the
critical activity of his vigorous mind. From the spirit of
the age whose literature he loved Byron learned early to suspect something unsound in sectarian strife, and straightway
abjured dogmatism. His repudiation of traditional beliefs
began in his earliest verse, not as atheism, but as a defiant
attitude toward the accretions Christianity had gathered from
the interpretations put upon it by men. It was not a placid
indifference to traditional dogma, but a violent rejection of
the claims made by religious establishments to exclusive possession of authority in matters of belief.
     The youthful _Prayer of Nature_, which Byron withheld
from publication during his lifetime,[23] reveals much that
later became characteristic of Byron. Saturated with the
temper of the eighteenth century, it is his first complete
avowal of 'natural' as opposed to 'revealed' religion. Here
he first attempts to throw off childhood beliefs, the teaching that all must perish 'for one who fell,' and that the
penalty of disbelief is damnation. And in this youthful ef-
fusion comes the first evidence of his challenge to the
forces of orthodoxy, to 'bigots,' 'superstitition,' and
'mystic rites.' It is the beginning of his divergence from
all religious authority.
     There is almost nothing in the poem to limit the

----

[20]Note to _Childe Harold_, iii, st. 91, v. 3 (1816).

[21]_Letters_, II, 18 ff. (1811); cf. _Hints from Horace_, vv. 373-382 (1811);
Childe Harold, ii, st. 3 (1812); _op. cit._, iii, st. 43 (1816); _Don Juan_,
i, st. 83 (1818); _Deformed Transformed_, II.iii.(1822).

[22]'Why do these exist to perplex and puzzle the mind?' he later asked
Kennedy; 'and does it not seem a fair conclusion,--let it alone, and let
these people fight among themselves, and when they have settled what religion is, then we can begin to study it.'--Kennedy, p. 188 (1823); cf.
Don Juan, ix, st. 16, vv. 5-6 (1822).

[23]Moore found the MS among the papers entrusted to him in preparation
for the _Life and Letters_, q. v., Chapter V.

application of its skepticism to any one sect. He was turning
away, not only from Calvinism, but from formulated creeds of
all kinds. Hence the indiscriminateness of his next outburst,
the letter to Ensign Long: 'Of Religion I know nothing, at
least in its favour. We have fools in all sects and Impostors
in most; why should I believe mysteries no one understands,
because written by men who chose to mistake madness for Inspiration, and style themselves Evangelicals?. . . . I have
lived a Deist, what I shall die I know not; however, come what
may, ridens moriar.'[24] The following year he wrote to Dallas
'a brief compendium of the sentiments of the wicked George,
Lord Byron; and, till I get a new suit, you will perceive I
am badly cloathed.'[25] After the period occupied by his work
on English Bards, the addresses in Parliament, and the first
pilgrimage, began the intercourse with Harness and Hodgson
which culminated in the letters to Hodgson.[26] Then came the
publication of Childe Harold, with its tirades against ecclesiastical systems all and sundry:

> Here the red cross (for still the cross is here,
> Though sadly scoff'd at by the circumcised)
> Forgets that pride to pamper'd priesthood dear,--
> Churchman and votary alike despised.
> Foul Superstition! howsoe'er disguised,
> Idol, saint, virgin, prophet, crescent, cross,
> For whatsoever symbol thou art prized,
> Thou sacerdotal gain, but general loss!
> Who from true worship's gold can separate they dross?
>   Childe Harold, ii, st. 44 (1812)[27]

The theatricality of Harold's declamations against
'pamper'd priesthood,' quite comparable to the turgid style of
the earlier letters, immediately calls up a doubt whether such
outbursts are to be interpreted as sincere statements of opinion or whether they are employed for the mere joy of shocking
the orthodox. Certainly one evidence of Byron's immaturity is
the posturing in these early poems and letters; he was quite
aware that the role of a religious skeptic was a most apt addition to the drama he conceived his life to be. But despite
all his straining aftereffect, there are characteristics of
Byron's true nature evident in all these declarations of
hostility to the orthodox tradition. He denies the power of

---

[24]Letters, II, 19 (1807). It was during this year that he wrote out
the list of books he had read, and declared his independence of 'absurd
and damnable heresies, mysteries, and Thirty-nine Articles.'

[25]Letters, I, 172 (1808).

[26]The letters are too long to be quoted entire here. See Letters, II,
18 ff., 34 ff. (1811).

[27]See also ibid., stanzas 3, 7, and 8.

'Galileeism' to elevate human life;[28] he rejects the authority of the Scriptures,[29] and voices passionate opposition to
all religious establishments. At the same time, there persists steadily his belief in the existence of a Creator, and
his attitude of 'true worship' despite the intervention of
priestly authority. He confesses that the rejection of tradition occasions him distress.[30] His skepticism is hence not
totally irreconcilable with the reflections of traditional
teaching discussed in the foregoing· chapter. There are admittedly vacillations and inconsistencies; but they are not
of so vital a nature as to invalidate the conclusion that
Byron was skeptical of creeds which he considered man-made,
but that in his expression of disbelief there is a note of
agitation caused by the powerful influence which historic
dogmas exercised upon his imagination.

The persistent skepticism in Byron's poetry was hence
not an affectation of cynicism. Could he have accepted whole-
heartedly any system of religious belief or any satisfactory
heresy, it seems more likely than not that he would have done
so. It was rather the irrepressible activity of a mind which
stubbornly applied itself to the grounds of doubt and belief.
'If I valued fame, I should flatter received opinions, which
have gathered strength by time, and will yet wear longer than
any living works to the contrary. But, for the soul of me, I
cannot and will not give the lie to my own thoughts and doubts,
come what may. If I am a fool, it is, at least, a doubting
one; and I envy no one the certainty of his self-approved
wisdom.' [31]

This is the significance of a statement quoted before:

[28]See _Letters_, II, 18 ff. Cf. _Childe Harold_, ii, st. 44 (quoted
above): 'sacerdotal gain but general loss.'

[29]See letter to Long, _Letters_, II, 19 (1807): 'mysteries no one understands'; _Letters_, II, 34 ff. (1811): 'I do not believe in any revealed
religion, because no religion is revealed'; _Letters_, III, 403 (1813): 'If
I do not at present place implicit faith in tradition and revelation of
any human creed, I hope it is not from want of reverence for the Creator
but the created.' Byron always vacillated about the credibility of the
Scriptures; he employed Genesis for _Cain_ as though he were willing to consider it authoritative, but his defense in the Preface to _Cain_ is not calculated to convince one of his orthodoxy in a literal sense. See _Don
Juan_, xi, st. 4 (1822): '_no one_ ever could decide.'

[30]See original MS of _Childe Harold_, ii, st. 8 (1811-12), reprinted in
Poetical Works II:

> Frown not upon me, churlish Priest! that I
> Look not for Life, where life may never be;
> I am no sneerer at thy phantasy;
> Thou pitiest me,--alas! I envy thee.

[31]_Letters_, II, 351-2, 'Journal,' [Nov.] 27, 1813.

'To have no religion at all! all sense, and senses, are
against it; but all belief and much evidence is for it.'[32]
It is Byron's characteristically loose description of what he
took to be two distinct types of mental activity. The rationalistic tendencies of his mind ("sense, and senses") led
to skepticism; but the faculty which romantic psychology would
designate 'feeling' or 'intuition' in distinction to 'knowledge' (he calls it 'belief') tended toward the acceptance of
ideas which could not sustain the examination of his critical
reflection. He was a romanticist in religion.[33]

The spontaneous activity of critical reason was hence
a constant factor in Byron's philosophizing. It is the explanation of his continual attempts to break down the body of
dogma which oppressed him. To his quick bosom there could
never come the quiet of indifference. That was why he took
up the study of Armenian: 'I found that my mind wanted something craggy to break upon.'[34]

This is the nerve and sinew of Manfred. A mind that
will not be stilled, a courage that outfaces Arimanes on his
throne, and a passionate sense of individuality are voiced in
the disdainful defiance of Manfred. The lone watcher of Alpine immensities has won a spiritual strength which exults in
unaided battle with the powers that limit him. It is Byron's
first major struggle with the problem of sin, and he as-
saults it single-handed. Christianity? It offers aid in the
words of the abbot,[35] and puny indeed is its proffered strength
beside the power of the individual mind:

> Old man! there is no power in holy men,
> Nor charm in prayer, nor purifying form
> Of penitence, nor outward look, nor fast,
> Nor agony, nor, greater than all these,

[32] Correspondence, II, 46 (1817).

[33] For his own expression of the necessity of subordinating the rationalistic tendencies of the mind in order to achieve belief cf. Don
Juan, xvi, st. 5-6:

> But Saint Augustine has the great priority,
>   Who bids all men believe the impossible,
> Because 't is so. Who nibble, scribble, quibble, he
>   Quiets at once with 'quia impossible.'

Galt, p. 268 made the same observation: 'Lord Byron had but loose feelings in religion--scarcely any. His sensibility and a slight constitu-
tional leaning towards superstition and omens showed that the sense of devotion was, however, alive and awake within him; but with him religion was
a sentiment, and the convictions of the understanding had nothing whatever
to do with his creed.'

[34] Letters, IV, 9-10 (1816).

[35] See Chew, Dramas, Chap. IV.

> The innate tortures of that deep despair,
> Which is remorse without the fear of hell
> But all in all sufficient to itself
> Would make a hell of heaven,--can exorcise
> From out the unbounded spirit the quick sense
> Of its own sins, wrongs, sufferance, and revenge
> Upon itself; there is no future pang
> Can deal that justice on the self-condemn'd
> He deals on his own soul.
>
> Manfred, III.i.66-78 (1817).

The repudiation of traditional religion is the outcome of youthful philosophizing. If skepticism is not the major theme of Manfred, it is only because here Byron totally ignores the Christian tradition. It is to be remembered that the third act of Manfred was rewritten at the advice of Shelley. Here, as in the pantheism of Childe Harold, is traceable the influence of 'a man of a perfectly modern and perfectly emancipated mind.' [36] And it is worth noting that, just as the sense of personal reality made Byron balk at the surrender of self implied in the historic doctrines of original sin and vicarious atonement, so here it is the passionate individualism of Manfred which spurns the aid of Christianity. Byron never developed a systematic philosophy of religion which would answer his continual questioning of the means to salvation. He never decided whether the power to avert the consequences of sin resided with man or not. But sin and its consequences were not the less real for that; and in Manfred personal defiance, not traditional religion, is opposed to the evil principle. Here Byron is almost unique. Personal responsibility for sin concerns the Christian more than the Hellenist. Byron offers as counterpart, not the Christian system of grace, but the defiance of Prometheus. His sense of sin is Christian; his attitude toward the consequences is Greek, or at least Shelleyan.

This dilemma is the essence of Prometheus (1816). Man's 'sad unallied existence' gives him only one power, the power to oppose patient courage to divine displeasure. The human spirit is 'triumphant where it dares defy.' An orthodox Christian could never have written those lines, for they utterly ignore the power of Divine grace operating in the heart of man to avert the consequences of evil.

Byron's skepticism of the authoritative Christian tradition suffers no interruption, even during the period when pantheism appeared most abundantly in his poetry. He was intellectually ready for Cain in 1817. It is plausible to suppose that the biblical dramas were in a certain sense delayed by a temporary preoccupation with pantheism and with the

---

[36]Brandes, p. 300.

historical dramas. But this is not to say that pantheism sup-
planted the old strife of doubt and belief in Byron. The
theories of Shelley, of Lucretius, of Erasmus Darwin and
Cuvier, took their place in his thoughts beside the preexist-
ing and persistent beliefs, but did not supplant them. The
development of Byron's mind was almost wholly additive.

So much has been written about Cain that any discussion of the drama must take as a point of departure analyses
which already treat the subject in thoroughly adequate fashion.[37] Most commentators agree that in Cain Byron impugned
the doctrines which Christianity has erected upon the events
narrated in Genesis. Byron could not reconcile predestination, the doctrine of original sin, and the curse placed upon
mankind, with the idea of a just or loving Deity. Both the
major characters, Cain and Lucifer, affirm that God is just
only in the sense that his acts are arbitrarily exempted from
all distinctions of good and evil.[38] Divine sovereignty is
represented as antecedent to and subversive of divine good-
ness. Neither within the limits of the play, nor in the letters which he wrote to defend himself against the consequent
charges of moral culpability, did he attempt to disprove the
utterances of Lucifer and Cain.

No matter whether or not the specific criticisms of
Christianity advanced in Cain were Byron's personal convictions, the fact remains that he presented an indictment of
orthodox religious tradition. It was a courageous act in
that day; the literal credibility of Genesis is no longer a
matter of paramount concern to religious or philosophical
thought, but at that time it was deemed a crucial point.
British orthodoxy was outraged. 'The parsons are all preach-
ing at it,' he wrote Moore, 'from Kentish Town and Oxford to
Pisa,--the scoundrels of priests, who do more harm to religion than all the infidels that ever forgot their cate-
chisms!'[39] And he maintained doggedly that he was not seeking to attack religion. 'I am no enemy to religion, but the
contrary. . . .I think people can never have enough religion,
if they are to have any.'[40] Yet in Cain he pointed out that a

---

[37]Dr. Chew's admirable discussion (Dramas of Lord Byron) is prere-
quisite to any serious study. Brandes is particularly valuable in ap-
praising the significance of Cain for Kulturgeschichte. Stopford Brooke's
excellent and apparently little-known article (Hibbert Journal, XVIII) is
probably the best presentation of the theological background of the drama.
It is unlikely that anything yet to be written will supersede these.
Richter (pp. 392-3) has presented more conclusive evidence than anyone
else that many avowals of belief in Cain are Byron's own. Donner and
Eimer both interpret the drama as evidence of their respective theses.

[38]See Cain, I..ii.648-651, and III.i.246-247.

[39]Letters, VI, 23-4 (1822).

[40]Letters, VI, 31-33 (1822); for the other letters in defense of Cain
see op. cit., V, 368, 469-470; op. cit., VI, 13 ff., 23-24.

logical interpretation of traditional dogma resulted in a hate-
ful conception of the Divine Nature--a•conception at variance
with his profound feeling of reverence. It is indeed possible
to interpret Cain as an implicit denial of the truth of dogmas
that lead to such a conclusion.[41] On the other hand, it is
perfectly evident from the testimony of Byron's associates and
from his own confession that these dogmas seemed to him to
have at least some degree of validity; Cain must therefore not
be taken as a clear-cut statement of belief or disbelief. It
is rather a portrayal of the emotional and intellectual confusion which Byron had experienced, and of which he never completely rid himself. Cain learns, indeed, that man is evil--
'I am awake at last'--but to Adah's final words, 'Peace be
with him!' he can only reply, 'But with me!'

        Byron could certainly have foreseen that the forces of
orthodoxy would misunderstand totally his speculations about
the origin and nature of evil when presented in the form which
he adopted. For he seemed to glorify the power of evil by a
sympathetic portraiture of Lucifer; hence Southey's characterization of his poetry as 'Satanic.' The adjective is not un-
suited to Byron's poetry if it be restricted to mean a keen
and sympathetic interest in the Devil and his attributes. In
addition to Arimanes in Manfred, the Devil appears in propria
persona in The Devil's Drive (1813), The Vision of Judgment
(1821), Cain (1821), and The Deformed Transformed (1822);
there are also distributed throughout all his other works a
surprisingly large number of allusions to Satan.[42] The extreme interest which Byron took in the doctrine of original
sin had no doubt excited his interest in the Satanic tradition; and it should be noted that his diabolism in all the
minor allusions and in the weaker extended poems, The Devil's
Drive and Heaven and Earth, is largely traditional. But Byron,
influenced no doubt by what he considered to be a relatively
independent treatment of tradition in Paradise Lost,[43] showed
a strong tendency to experiment with the Devil as dramatis
persona. In the Deformed Transformed he employed a Goethean
conception recognizably influenced by Mephistopheles; the

        [41]See note to Don Juan, xv, st. 18: 'I mean by "Diviner still," Christ.
If ever God was man--or man God--he was both. I never arranged his creed,
but the use--or abuse--made of it.' (1823)
        [42]See Letters, I, 168 (1808), 293 (1810), 310 (1811); Correspondence,
I, 159 (1813), 243 (1814); Letters, V, 92 (1820); Don Juan, v, st. 109
(1820); Letters, V, 235 (1821); Don Juan, xi, st. 6 (1822); Letters, VI,
195 (1823); for references to the other fallen angels, see Correspondence,
I, 137 (1813); Letters, II, 351-2 (1813); Giaour, vv. 62-65 (1813); Don
Juan, iv, st. 1 (1819); Letters, V, 92 (1820); Heaven and Earth, I.iii.
828-859 (1821); Kennedy, pp. 50-51, 144-147, 154 (1823). See also below
for interest in Manicheism.
        [43]Medwin, pp. 47-48 (1821-2).

execution is weak and the characterization unimpressive. Simi-
larly, the Zoroastrianism employed in Manfred is certainly an
evidence of Byron's freedom in pursuing his heretical bent,
but in circumscribing the power of Arimanes by 'that which is
above him' Byron stops short of the thorough-going dualism of
Cain.[44] But the latter drama does not present a dualism of
good and evil in the original sense of the Manichaeans; in
Cain the opposition of the two ruling personalities implies no
ethical antithesis. To Byron, the Devil had become rather the
principle opposed to authoritarianism. Although Byron received the tradition from Christianity, he finally employed
it in a sense utterly foreign to the historic doctrine. In
The Vision of Judgment the personality of Lucifer is contrasted with orthodox stupidity; in Cain, Lucifer represents
not evil but knowledge.[45] The traditional machinery is completely unhinged. Good and evil are in the province of Divine
will; but the opposition of God and Lucifer is the opposition
of enforced ignorance and the will to knowledge.[46] The better
to scorn orthodoxy, Byron deliberately cultivated his incipient
diabolism; he almost always alluded to the Devil with a show
of mocking wit, or of cynical defiance toward tradition. 'He
was a fine fellow once, you know.'[47] Byron championed Lucifer
just as he championed Napoleon; toward both of them he felt a
sympathetic interest because he considered them maligned by
the forces of reaction and conservatism. By rejecting entirely the traditional identification of Lucifer with evil he implied a complete break with historic Christianity.

[44]Cain employs the Manichaean heresy, for which Byron seemed to have
an especial fondness, but there is no sound evidence for thinking that
he ever seriously accepted it. Professor Chew (Dramas, Chapters IV and
VII) has shown that the Manichaeism was objective, and not personal.
But Byron's prepossession with the belief must be recognized, and interpreted as an evidence of his predilection for a dualistic conception of
moral values. See also other evidences of Byron's interest in the heresy:
Letters, II, 78 and note 1 (1811), 83 (1811); op. cit., V, 54 and note 2
(1820), 391-2 (1821); Medwin, p. 50, p. 86 (1821-2); Don Juan, vi, st. 3
(1822); op. cit., xiii, st. 41 (1823).

[45]Critics are in virtual agreement on this point. See particularly
Schaffner, Greef, and Wenzel. Brandes, Chapter XX, has a good discussion. Chew, Chapter VII, Eimer pp.188-192, and Ackermann, Kaptel VI,
should be carefully consulted.

[46]Hence Heber's attack in the Quarterly Review. Byron is charged with
having transferred 'from God to Satan and from Satan to God, the qualities by which, in the general estimation of mankind, they are most distinguished from each other.' The distinctive qualities cited by the irate
Bishop were sympathy with man and justice, which Byron gives to Lucifer;
whereas Byron assigns to God tyranny over nature, capricious destruction,
and avidity of worship.—p. 515.

[47]Letters, V, 92 (1820).

It is evident from the foregoing that Byron was deeply concerned with doubts about Christian doctrine from earliest manhood until the full fruition of his powers in Cain and Don Juan. Side by side with his belief in the existence of a personal God, and paralleling his constant preoccupation with theological dogma, there runs the current of thought which tends constantly to deny that the supernatural enters into relation with man or that human experience is explicable by accepted modes of religious belief. He manifests his skepticism in generalized hostility to the claim of Christianity to the possession of absolute truth. Opposition to authoritarian absolutism is a constant element of his thought at all times. Some account must also be taken of his explicit denial of specific tenets of Christianity, particularly his denial of the existence of Hell and the expectation of a personal survival.

Byron's rejection of the doctrine of everlasting punishment may be dismissed summarily because all commentators agree that it is a constant element of Byron's verse and prose. His reasoning on the subject was erratic and cloudy, but it is sufficient to say that he denied the existence of Hellfire because it seemed to him incompatible with the concept of a benign Deity.[48] In more violent moods of disbelief he repudiated entirely the theological systems upon which the doctrine is based.[49]

But this rejection of the Athanasian anathema must be understood, not as complacent indifference, but as an extremely alert reiteration of disbelief, which shows his uneasiness upon the subject. 'Against one dogma only he never varied in his denunciations--the eternity of hell torments,' writes Elze. 'Had he really been convinced of "eternal sleep," this doctrine would necessarily have been indifferent to him; it was, on the contrary, dreaded by him, and he found something consolatory and seductive in the Catholic doctrine of Purgatory; indeed, he was not without leanings toward the Church of Rome.'[50] Byron's denial of the reality of Hell is the result of an inner conflict in which dread, belief, and incredulity played their part; here his skepticism faced an issue with a high emotional content which betrays the intensity of the inward struggle.

---

[48]Prayer of Nature, vv. 21-24 (1806); Letters, II, 19 (1807); op. cit., V, 457 (1821).

[49]See Poetical Works, I, 484, note 1 (1813); Correspondence, II, 155 (1820); Letters, V, 51 (1820); Vision of Judgment, st. xiii, st. xiv (1821); Letters, VI, 35-6 (1822); Don Juan, viii, st. 26, st. 114 (1822); Elze, p. 482; Blessington, p. 302 (1823).

[50]Elze, p. 365.

Byron's intense interest in the existence of Hell is
of course immediately related to his constant pondering upon
the question of immortality. His early period of orthodox belief and its occasional recurrence have already been men-
tioned. As the belief in a personal survival weakened, he
tended more and more to entertain the idea that death would be
followed by extinction. The influences which led him to aban-
don his former faith in a personal immortality were active
very early in life, for his skepticism is traceable in the
earliest poems.[51] He later wrote to Gifford: 'It was the
comparative insignificance of ourselves and our world, when
placed in competition with the mighty whole, of which it is an
atom, that first led me to imagine that our pretensions to
eternity might be over-rated.'[52] The correspondence between
this belief and the note of despair in Byron's poetry is easily apparent, but is probably accidental rather than a product
of systematic philosophizing. The appropriateness of the
idea of death to the illustration of the transience of earthly
endeavor is so perfectly obvious that one would be surprised
were the Byron of the earlier Childe Harold to ignore it.

It is useless to assign precise chronological limitations to the appearance of the theme of annihilation. The
first note is sounded in 1806; in the first draft of Childe
Harold (ii, st. 8) he made his last dogmatic denial of personal immortality; and Lara is the last poem prior to the
emergence of pantheistic reveries in which the longing for a
dreamless sleep occurs. It is enough to say that Byron's
early orthodoxy waned after 1806; in that year he showed the
earliest evidence of a belief in extinction, which continued
until about the time of the second departure from England.[53]
The appearance of pantheistic beliefs in Byron's

[51]See Prayer of Nature (1806), vv. 57-58:

But, if this fleeting spirit share
With clay the grave's eternal bed. . . .

[52]Letters, II, 221-222 (1813). Cf. Letters, III, 408 (1814): 'Why I
came here I know not. Where I shall go to, it is useless to inquire. In
the midst of myriads of the living and the dead worlds - stars—systems—
infinity why should I be anxious about an atom?'

[53]See also Donner, pp. 51-52, 99 ff., 109 ff.; and Eimer, pp. 46, 21-23,
for comparison with foregoing. Donner places too much emphasis upon the
relation between Byron's belief in annihilation at death and his characteristic gloom and misanthropy. Eimer is interested primarily in the
evidences of scientific study. See also The Adieu, vv. 8-10 and 101-103,
for a good example of Byron's habit of self-contradiction (1807); In-
scription on a Monument (1808); Letters, I, 172 (1808); op. cit., II, 18
ff., 36 (1811); And Thou Art Dead (1812); Euthanasia (publ. 1812); Childe
Harold, ii, st. 4, 5, 7, 8 (original draft), 39, 53 (1812); Giaour,
1269-1270, 994-995 (1813); Letters, II, 351-2 (1813).

poetry involves a change in his speculations about the immortality of the soul. It implies a rejection of the claim
of Christianity to authoritative teaching. In the degree to
which Byron approached completely pantheistic beliefs he
broke with traditional doctrine. But more important to an
understanding of Byron's withdrawal from Christianity is the
tendency of his later years toward agnostic or skeptic attitudes,[54] one phase of which is his denial that there can be
any reliable means of investigating the nature of death. His
earlier avowals of belief in personal annihilation at death
were essentially a denial of the ability of consciousness to
bridge the apparent gap between life and that which may follow it. Even under the influence of pantheistic thought,
when he seemed to accept a belief in immortality, he did not
maintain that the consciousness which might follow death would
be in any way comparable to that of earthly life. Hence,
pantheism did not lead him to affirm that which he had earlier
denied, the continuity of personality beyond death.[55] It follows that his later denial of the attainability of knowledge
about death is but another aspect of the earlier beliefs:
consciousness, as we understand it, cannot extend its faculties of apprehension beyond the moment of death; hence we
have no knowledge of the nature of death.

It should be noted in this connection that expressions
leading to the position of agnosticism are present in his
earlier poetry, but are so inconspicuous as to constitute little more than chance notes. [56] After the first pantheistic
rapture had somewhat subsided, Byron's doubts began to assert
themselves more forcibly in forms which led to the agnostic or

[54]This is one of the chief divergences between Donner's investigation
and Eimer's. The former (Chapter VII) maintains that Byron's final position was skepticism. Eimer, emphasizing Byron's study of natural sciences
rather than his metaphysical speculations, substitutes the positive results of such pursuits as the dominant theme (pp. 170, 187-189).

[55]See Donner, pp.108-109, and Eimer, p. 169.

[56]See I Would I Were a Careless Child, vv. 17-24 (1808); Letters, II,
18-19, for the 'absurdity' of speculating on another life (1811); Letters,
II, 384-385: 'Is there anything beyond? who knows? He that can't tell.
Who tells that there is? He who don't know.'(1814); Childe Harold, ii,
st. 7: 'All that we know is, nothing can be known' (1812). See also his
undated letter from Venice: 'My opinion is that I shall live beyond my
reputation, as you have done, though perhaps variously, or both, and expect no better end than the ocean for the reception of my body, and sun
or moon (God wot) for my soul. I cannot lawfully or logically look for
more, and if in another life I am united to those I love, I shall be
fortunate in my decease, which is more than I have reason to expect'
(Seventeen Letters, p. 46). From the same volume comes the statement:
. . . I have little hope of happiness on earth, and no expectation of
attaining it hereafter' (p. 49).

skeptic position. The <u>Ode on Venice</u> certainly implies that
Byron was tending, in certain characteristic moods, toward
agnosticism:

> . . . .the last rattle chokes the strangled scream,
> And all is ice and blackness,--and the earth
> That which it was the moment ere our birth.
> vv. 53-55 (1818).

There is no indication here of any insight into the nature of
death; it is rather a denial of any continuity of consciousness between the present and the hereafter. <u>Cain</u>, too, shows
that Byron felt himself unable to attain an imaginative experience symbolic or suggestive of the nature of death:

> These dim realms!
> I see them, but I know them not.
> <u>Cain</u>, II.ii.372-373.

<u>This</u> is essentially the skepticism of <u>Sardanapalus</u>.
The representation of the Assyrian monarch, although not a
deliberate confession of faith, is in large measure a speci-
men of Byronic self-portraiture. Like Sardanapalus, Byron had
denied the power of priests, had held death to be extinction,
and had abjured the traditional faith of his fathers. Simi-
larly, he had wondered if death might not lead to higher knowledge (IV.i.52-3), and had at moments admitted by implication
that belief in a personal survival was an alternative possibility. The protean nature of Byron's mind is the true significance of <u>Sardanapalus</u>. The drama is an incomplete and
sketchy reflection of certain conflicting aspects of the
poet's mind: sensualism, pacifism, adoration of nature, and
unsteady skepticism of religious tradition.[57]
The evidence that <u>Cain</u> and <u>Sardanapalus</u> have autobiographical significance is contained in the letters and in
the reflective digressions of <u>Don Juan</u>. His prepossession
with the problem of immortality is repeatedly avowed:

> But still the spouseless virgin <u>Knowledge</u> flies.
> What are we? and whence came we? what shall be

---

[57]See Donner, p. 109, and Eimer, p. 156 ff. Eimer gives far too much
prominence to the positive naturalistic content at the expense of the
skepticism in the drama; his treatment is based upon II.i.1-36, 62-80,
236-268, 311-312, 345-349; III.i.275-283; V.i.1-56, 450. Donner sees the
play as a <u>Glaubensbekentniss</u>. See, in addition to the foregoing, the
passages which seem to show Byron's wavering between doubt and belief:
I.ii.591-595, 610-613; III.i.155-160; IV.i.52-53; V.i.159-160, 405-409,
422 ff.

> Our <u>ultimate</u> existence? what's our present?
> Are questions answerless, and yet incessant.
> <u>Don Juan</u>, vi, st. 63 (1822)[58]

At moments he returns to the older belief that death
results in annihilation,[59] or declares that man's hopes of a
future existence is mere egotism.[60] But Byron was seldom dogmatic in these last years. The uncertain light of his 'versified aurora borealis' shines momentarily from almost every
quarter, and nothing remains long in sharp relief:

> The path is through perplexing ways, and when
> The goal is gain'd, we die, you know--and then--

> What then?--I do not know, no more do you--
>   And so good night.
> <u>Don Juan</u>, i, st. 133-134 (1818).[61]

The latest stage of Byron's search for truth was
marked by almost every form of skepticism which had characterized his thinking in earlier years. But in addition to
the earlier ideas, there appeared an increasing preoccupation
with the theory of knowledge which requires special consideration. Byron was not becoming a critical epistemologist; but
intellectual maturity had brought with it a more acute and
persistent attention to the problem of knowledge than is elsewhere evident in his poetry.

Precise chronological limitations are of course un-
safe. In so far as the last stage of Byron's skepticism is a
continuation of earlier processes of thought, there is no
sharp line of demarcation. On the other hand, the bitter
irony of <u>Cain</u> and <u>Don Juan,</u> and the mocking laughter of <u>Beppo</u>
and the <u>Vision of Judgment</u>, are certainly to be distinguished
from the dolorous affectation which lingers in the last two
cantos of <u>Childe Harold</u>. When the despair consequent upon his
exile from England had somewhat abated, and when he had begun

---

[58]See also <u>Don Juan</u>, xiv, st. v-vi: 'the lurking bias. . . .To the <u>un-known</u>' (1823); <u>Don Juan</u>, xv, st. 91 (1823):

> I always knock my head against some angle
> About the present, past, or future state.

[59]<u>Don Juan</u>, iv, st. 12: 'the silent shore' (1819); <u>op. cit</u>., xi, st.
4 (1822); <u>Letters</u>, VI, 56-57 (on the death of Allegra): 'she is either
at rest or happy' (1822); <u>Don Juan</u>, xiv, st. 4: 'a sleep without
dreams. . . .is what we covet most' (1823).

[60]See <u>Letters</u>, V, 186-187 (1821); cf. <u>op. cit</u>., VI, 36: 'they think
themselves so <u>important</u> in the creation, that nothing less can satisfy
their pride—the insects' (1822).

[61]Cf. <u>Don Juan</u>, ii, st. 134: 'God only knows' (1819); <u>op. cit</u>., v. st.
38-39: 'Here we are, And there we go:--but <u>where</u>?' (1820). Cf. <u>Letters</u>,
V, 190 (1821).

to assimilate the spirit of Italian culture, it would be
strange were not his reflections upon the meaning and value
of his fresh experience stimulated and otherwise enriched by
an expanding intellectual horizon. In the period marked by
these somewhat vague limitations, and particularly during the
composition of Don Juan, Byron's skepticism was expressed
with a higher degree of acumen and penetration than in any of
his previous poetry.

Byron's intellectual maturity was attended by increased
awareness of the leading philosophical and religious thought
of his age. Hence his critical attitude toward theories of
knowledge corresponds to that movement toward idealistic
philosophy which runs through Berkeley and Kant, and is further developed by the German philosophers who followed them
in criticism of epistemological theories. This is not to say
that Byron was conversant with these philosophers, nor that
he was directly influenced by them. But it is quite evident
that Byron's attention was turning more and more to speculations which won for the contemporary movement in philosophical
thought the designation 'idealism.'

Byron was in part prepared to recognize that many
ideas have only a subjective validity by his early attention
to the disagreements of religious sects. The violence of
their disputes occupied his attention all through his life.[62]
The mutual inconsistencies of sects led him naturally to the
rationalistic comparison of philosophical systems, and there-
upon to the rejection of dogmatism.

> Therefore I would solicit free discussion
>   Upon all points--no matter what, or whose--
> Because as Ages upon Ages push on,
>   The last is apt the former to accuse
> Of pillowing its head on a pin-cushion,
>   Heedless of pricks because it was obtuse:
> What was a paradox becomes a truth or
> A something like it--witness Luther!
>   Don Juan, xvii, st. 6 (1823-4).

'Paradox,' 'truth or something like it'--these became
Byron's latest definitions of knowledge. He was tending
steadily toward the evolutionary concept that truth is not

[62]See Don Juan, xv, st. 89 (1823):

> But what's reality? Who has its clue?
> Philosophy? No: she too much rejects.
> Religion? Yes; but which of all her sects?

Cf. Letters, VI, 388 (1821); Medwin, p. 48 (1821-2); Aristomenes, Poetical
Works, IV, 566 (1823).

static but dynamic or developmental:

> One system eats another up, and this
>   Much as old Saturn ate his progeny;
>   . . . .
> But System doth reverse the Titan's breakfast,
>   And eats her parents, albeit the digestion
> Is difficult.
>   Don Juan, xiv, st. 1-2 (1823).[63]

With the developmental conception of truth Byron associated his profound distrust of the ability of the human mind to comprehend absolute knowledge:

> And, after all, what is a lie? 't is but
>   The truth in masquerade; and I defy
> Historians, heroes, lawyers, priests, to put
>   A fact without some leaven of a lie.
> The very shadow of true Truth would shut
>   Up annals, revelations, poesy,
> And prophecy--except it should be dated
> Some years before the incidents related.
>   Don Juan, xi, st. 37 (1822)[64]

Hence doubt seemed to him a necessary component of belief. The idealistic conception of the development of human knowledge as a three-fold process (thesis, antithesis, synthesis) abandons the definition of doubt as negation, emphasizing rather its corrective or purgative function.[65] The

---

[63]Cf. Don Juan, xv, st. 90 (1823):

> 'T is time that some new prophet should appear,
>   Or old indulge man with a second sight.
> Opinions wear out in some thousand years,
>   Without a small refreshment from the spheres.

[64]Cf. Don Juan, xi, st. 2 (1822): "Heaven's brandy, though our brain can hardly bear it." Cf. Letters, VI, 89 (1822).

[65]See Don Juan, ix, st. 17 (1822):

> "So little do we know what we're about in
>   This world, I doubt if doubt itself be doubting.

Cf. Don Juan, xi, st. 2 (1822):

> Oh Doubt!--if thou be'st Doubt, for which some take thee,
> But which I doubt extremely--thou sole prism
> Of the Truth's rays. . . .

Cf. Blessington, p. 169 (1823): 'I think it was Luther who said that the human mind was like a drunken man on horseback,' said Byron to the Countess; '--prop it on one side, and it falls on the other. . . .' Cf. Childe Harold, iv, st. 130 (1818): 'Time!. . . .The test of truth, love, --sole philosopher.'

abandonment of a dogmatic faith that the universe is established on logical principles implies that the laws of identity and contradiction are no longer applicable:

> I will not swear that black is white;
> But I suspect in fact that white is black,
> And the whole matter rests upon eyesight.
> Ask a blind man, the best judge. You'll attack
> Perhaps this new position--but I'm right;
> Or if I'm wrong, I'll not be ta'en aback:--
> He hath no morn nor night, but all is dark
> Within; and what seest thou? A dubious spark.
> > Don Juan, xii, st. 71 (1823).

The subjective idealism implicit in the foregoing
stanza at once suggests Berkeley; there seems to be no reason
to doubt that Byron had some acquaintance with his philosophy.[66] The humorous cast of his stanzas on Berkeley [67] is not
to be mistaken for trifling; his jests about idealistic theories did not disturb the deeper current of brooding beneath.[68]
Byron was not a systematic devotee of idealism; but the deep
interest which he took in it explains in large measure his
distrust of the testimony of the senses:

> Nothing more true than not to trust your senses;
> And yet what are your other evidences?
> > Don Juan, xiv, st. 2 (1823)[69]

It is also to be remarked that Byron refers several
times to the Kantian doctrine that our ideas of space and

[66]Byron listed Berkeley as one of the philosophers he had read by 1807
(Moore, Chap. V).

[67]Don Juan, xi, st. 1-2 (1822).

[68]Don Juan, who was real, or ideal,--
> For both are much the same, since what men think
> Exists when the once thinkers are less real
> Than what they thought, for mind can never sink,
> And 'gainst the body makes a strong appeal;
> And yet 't is very puzzling on the brink
> Of what is call'd eternity, to stare,
> And know no more of what is here, than there;--
> > Don Juan, x, st. 20 (1822).

[69]Cf. Deformed Transformed, I.ii.582-5 (1822):

> Caes: Because you know no better than the dull
> And dubious notice of your eyes and ears.
> Arn. I'll trust them.
> Caes.   Do! they will deceive you sweetly,
> And that is better than the bitter truth.

time are not truly representative of objective reality, but a priori conditions of perception.[70]   Human ideas have only a subjective validity. From specific skepticism of religious tradition he has come to a skepticism which implies that the fruits of human reasoning are only suggestive or symbolic, not final.

> This is the consequence of giving matter
> The power of thought. It is a stubborn substance,
> And thinks chaotically, as it acts,
> Ever relapsing into its first elements.
> > Deformed Transformed, I.ii.884-887 (1822)

The matured poet comes to the problem of being in an alertly critical frame of mind. Pantheism has furnished no permanently satisfactory solution; realism has been abjured; and even the distinctions of identity and contradiction break down.

> 'To be, or not to be?'--Ere I decide,
>   I should be glad to know that which is being;
> 'T is true we speculate both far and wide,
>   And deem, because we see, we are all-seeing:
> For my part, I'll enlist on neither side,
>   Until I see both sides for once agreeing.
> For me, I sometimes think that life is death,
> Rather than life a mere affair of breath.
> > Don Juan, ix, st. 16 (1822)

The positive results of all Byron's pondering are slight. He has attained no new truth, nor has he adopted any satisfactory system. His only advance is a surer knowledge of the limits of human understanding. He now writes:

> I'm a philosopher; confound them all!
>   Bills, beasts, and men, and--no! not womankind!

[70]See Heaven and Earth, I.iii.566-573 (1821):

> Ay, day will rise; but upon what?--a chaos
> Which was ere day, and which, renew'd, makes time
> Nothing! for, without life, what are the hours?
> No more to dust than is eternity
> Unto Jehovah, who created both.
> Without him, even eternity would be
> A void: without man, time, as made for man,
> Dies with man.

Cf. Cain, II.i.161-165, 532-536; ibid., III.i.60-64; Letters, V, 309 (1821). Eimer, p. 163, shows that the idea may also have been taken from Lucretius, E. Darwin, or Young. Byron refers to Kant in Don Juan, x, st. 60, and in Devil's Drive, v. 202.

With one good hearty curse I vent my gall,
  And then my stoicism leaves nought behind
Which it can either pain or evil call,
  And I can give my whole soul up to mind;
Though what is soul or mind, their birth or growth,
Is more than I know--the deuce take them both!
                              Don Juan, vi, st. 22 (1822).

    The changes in Byron's mode of belief from his youth
to the time of his death do not represent the evolution of a
Weltanschauung. An earlier chapter has shown that the impress which the Christian tradition made upon his mind during
youth was ineradicable. To the very last he wondered if
'chance' or 'the old text' would ultimately prove to be the
explanation of this 'glorious blunder' called the world. His
skepticism followed a most tortuous path. Certain tendencies
can be selected as thematic: his hardy opposition to dogmatism, his idealism, or his beliefs about the nature of death.
But the mass is almost too heterogeneous for classification.
For example, during the last period of skepticism, there were
also present in his poetry many evidences that Byron believed in a certain type of immortality in which the soul was
thought to rejoin its original substance.[71] In view of the
extreme diversity of his opinions, and the peculiar constitu-
tion of a mind which could on two successive days honestly
avow mutually alien beliefs, it seems a priori unlikely that
Byron could ever attain a systematic philosophy. The maturing of his mind was not a critically selective synthesis of
converging beliefs, but a retentive accumulation of diverse
and often inconsistent ideas. New beliefs took their places
beside the old without supplanting them. Long after the theories of Cuvier had implied that Genesis was hardly an adequate
prologue to the drama of human life, he was brooding over its
opening chapters, and ranking side by side the words of Scripture and the speculations of palaeontologists. A statement
made earlier may perhaps be repeated: the development of his
mind was almost wholly additive. His philosophizing, like the
old play Tamburlaine, does not end; it merely stops.
    The proper understanding of Byron's poetry therefore
requires that the critic be prepared at any time to consider
the sincere statement of any one of several types of religious
or philosophical thought. Byron's psychological and emotional
type is not to be comprehended by a statement of his beliefs
or disbeliefs.
    With this caveat in mind, one may distinguish in the
course of Byron's development as a skeptic three major themes.
All his life, he opposed himself resolutely to absolutism in
any form; when it was presented to him in the nature of divine
authoritarianism, or in the form of fixed modes of religious

    [71]This will be discussed as a development of pantheistic ideas in the
following chapter.

or philosophical belief, he rebelled. This dogged persistence
in his 'own thoughts and doubts' manifested itself conspicuously in speculations concerning the nature of death; from early
maturity until the exile, he denied the Christian belief in
personal survival; and at all subsequent times he questioned
the power of earthly consciousness to extend its intellective
faculties beyond the moment of death. Finally, as the interest in pantheism subsided, he entered upon a period marked by
tendencies toward rationalistic idealism; this period was cut
short by death before any evidence of a synthesis of ideas appeared.

     This is the skepticism which so alarmed Byron's con-
temporaries. It represents the extreme limit of his reaction from Calvinistic teaching, and for the most part he
vacillated between the two. Although at times he took

                    a calm and shallow station
          Well nigh the shore[72]

his restless mind forbade more than a brief stay. 'Anything
but a dull cruise on a land lake,' he wrote.[73] His bark drove
on and on in a relentless but futile quest.

     In the wind's eye I have sail'd, and sail; but for
       The stars, I own my telescope is dim:
     But at least I have shunn'd the common shore,
       And leaving land far out of sight, would skim
     The ocean of eternity: the roar
       Of breakers has not daunted my slight, trim,
     But still sea-worthy skiff; and she may float
     Where ships have founder'd, as doth many a boat.
                    Don Juan, x, st. 4 (1822).

[72]Don Juan, ix, st. 18.
[73]Letters, III, 401.

Chapter Three

N A T U R A L I S M

With the stars
And the quick Spirit of the Universe
He held his dialogues; and they did teach
To him the magic of their mysteries;
To him the book of Night was open'd wide,
A marvel and a secret.

The Dream

The naturalism evident in much of Byron's poetry
should be taken into account in any attempt to explain the
vicissitudes of his poetic fame. His naturalism assumed many
forms, and in many instances it is quite probable that his
poetry won admiration or aroused censure according as it fell
upon ears prepared by an existent tradition to understand him
better than some of his contemporaries.

The poetry of Byron's early years and of the period
of his greatest vogue was rooted in the naturalistic tradi-
tions of the eighteenth century. Spinoza, Lucretius, Pope,
Rousseau, and Young were his earliest models, and a public
which found in at least a part of his verse nothing very different from that of writers to which it had long been ac-
customed accepted without alarm a great deal of his early
verse, not because it was original, but because it was imita-
tive. Although Byron's poetry seemed to deal with adventurous
lives exhausted by danger, riot, and dissipation, the thoughts
of the Byrónic hero and of Childe Harold were sometimes re-
assuringly commonplace. There is in reality much greater
originality in Wordsworth's best treatments of nature, because
his very definition of the words poetry and poet require that
expression arise from an inner fund of spiritual or aesthetic
power rather than from imitation.[1] But the spiritual insight
with which Wordsworth examined nature, unique as it may be,

---

[1]The poet 'is a man. . . . .endowed with more lively sensibility, more
enthusiasm and tenderness, who has a greater knowledge of human nature,
and a more comprehensive soul than are supposed to be common among mankind. . . .he has acquired a greater readiness and power in expressing
what he thinks and feels, and especially those thoughts and feelings
which, by his own choice, or from the structure of his own mind, arise
in him without immediate external excitement.'--'Preface.' Lyrical
Ballads.

naturally achieved slower recognition, particularly where its
simplicity, momentarily failing to achieve grandeur, seemed
trivial, and when its ethics, cloistering virtue in a north-
ern valley, seemed provincial. And just as Shelley had rejected all British tradition, religious, moral, and political,
so Britain rejected Shelley. For Shelley, nature is not necessarily English in its physical characteristics; nor yet universal, as Pope would interpret it; but unearthly, peculiarly
Shelleyan. Nor was England ready to accept Keats's sensuous
rendition of nature. That "trembling delicate and snail-horn
perception of beauty," of which he wrote to Benjamin Robert
Haydon[2] and which was his legacy to Tennyson, was not treas-
ured or rewarded until decades after his death. Whatever of
the classical mind remained in Keats's day rejected it, just as
in these days a critic of classic mold has dubbed such poets a
'petty, prying nature-cult.'[3]

Byron's dependence upon the existing tradition of
naturalism is most evident in his earliest work. He did not
remain wholly in that tradition; in fact, even before his
voluntary exile he had begun to cultivate interests which
later became so prominent that a second period beginning about
1816 may well be recognized. Five years later he began ener-
getically to elaborate ideas which had formerly been but an
undercurrent; hence we may recognize a third period beginning
about 1821. Too strict an application of such chronological
limits is utterly unwarranted; anticipations and recurrences
are to be expected. In general it will be found that the
first period is most obviously replete with imitations of
writers current in the preceding century; that in the second
he shows his closest approach to pantheism; and that in the
third the maturing of his intellectual power displayed itself
in restless activity amid a bewildering complexity of ideas
about science and its bearing on religion. One must first
consider the period depending on tradition.

I

INFLUENCES BEFORE SHELLEY

One cannot ignore, nor yet safely affirm, the

[2] Letter of April 8, 1818.

[3] Paul Elmer More, 'Biographical Sketch,' Poetical Works of Byron, p. xv.
Keats also perceived that Byron's acclaim was facilitated by his more objective (and hence more classical) touch: 'You speak of Lord Byron and me.
There is this great difference between us: he describes what he sees—I
describe what I imagine. Mine is the hardest task; now see the immense
difference. The Edinburgh Reviewers are afraid to touch upon my poem.
They do not know what to make of it. . . .'—Letter to George and Georgi-
ana Keats, Sept. 18, 1819.

influence of Spinoza upon Byron. He once declared that his
religious beliefs, in the main undecided, were 'verging towards Spinoza.'⁴ Although this statement seems to indicate
an immediate familiarity, there is no incontestable proof
that Byron ever read Spinoza's works. His acquaintance with
pantheistic thought must hence be traced to the currency of
such speculation among Byron's literary models wherever that
is possible.

Byron's indebtedness to Lucretius is well established.⁵
It is to be noted, however, that there is no certain evidence
of Lucretius' influence earlier than 1812, and that naturalism
in Byron's early poetry is therefore not originally related to
Lucretian doctrines.

Byron's dependence upon Pope is too well known to require much comment; it is clearly perceptible in Byron's early
religious poetry, and particularly in that professing a 'natural religion.' Pope's Essay on Man and Universal Prayer, as
formerly stated, furnished Byron with models of verse treat-
ing nature as an evidence of the wisdom and benevolence of the
divine plan, although Byron's imitations are frequently modified by his protests against the dogmas which he hated but
could not heartily disbelieve.

Similar to Byron's relation to Pope is his indebtedness to Rousseau. Since he began reading Rousseau at least
by the time he was sixteen, his tendency toward natural religion even during his earliest years may be attributed in part
to Rousseau's influence.⁶ It is to be remembered that Byron
was a voluminous reader possessed of an extremely retentive
memory, and that literature influenced by Rousseau had great
currency during the formative years of Byron's life. Except
in those cases in which verbal resemblances are close enough
to isolate indebtedness, as in his youthful imitations of
Pope, one is warranted only in attributing Byron's ideas to
the body of preceding literature taken as a whole.

Young, although not so important as Pope in his influence upon Byron, represents the tradition of meditative
devotional poetry which survives in some of Byron's early
poems. The argument from design, which reappears frequently
in Byron,⁷ is Young's forte. The latter is fond of such
themes as the solitude in nature which is not loneliness and

---

⁴Letters, II, 72 (1811). In 1821 Byron consented to put his name to a
translation of Spinoza projected by Shelley and Captain Williams; nothing
ever came of Byron's intended collaboration. See Buxton Forman, The Prose
Works of P. B. Shelley, 1880, IV, 312. Cf. also Donner, p. 113.

⁵See Fuhrmann,p. 86, and indices of Poetical Works.

⁶See Schmidt, Rousseau und Byron, p. 10 and pp. 91 ff.

⁷E. g.,Prayer of Nature, vv. 41-44 (1806): "Thou. . . .Whose hand
from pole to pole I trace." The idea is common in both Pope and Young.

the communication of man with earth and heavens.[8]   Thus Byron:

> To sit on rocks, to muse o'er flood and fell,
> To slowly trace the forest's shady scene,
> Where things that own not man's dominion dwell,
> And mortal foot hath ne'er or rarely been;
> To climb the trackless mountain all unseen,
> With the wild flock that never needs a fold;
> Alone o'er steeps and foaming falls to lean;
> This is not solitude, 't is but to hold
> Converse with Nature's charms and view her stores unroll'd.
>   Childe Harold, ii, st. 25 (1812).

The stanza here quoted offers a good example of the difficulty of making nice discriminations among Byron's sources, for despite the resemblance of the last two lines to Young, similarities have been traced to Wordsworth and Beattie as well.[9]   Beckford and Thomson must also be admitted to the list of Byron's masters, Beckford for turning Byron's attention to the existence of pantheistic cults among the Persians and Chaldeans,[10] and Thomson for passages resembling bits of the Seasons.[11]   It is evident that to seek every analogue for Byron's reflections upon nature and their religious implications is to complicate needlessly the statement that Byron was heavily indebted to the literature of the eighteenth century for his tendencies toward natural religion and pantheism.

Byron's interest in the development of the natural sciences also exerted a strong influence upon his thought.[12] Byron's awe of the infinitude of interstellar space had been vastly augmented by seeing 'myriads of the living and the dead worlds--stars--systems--infinity' through one of Herschel's

---

[8]Night Thoughts, Nights III and IX.

[9]Poetical Works II, 115, note 1.

[10]Beckford's Vathek pleased Byron mightily. Chew (in Dramas of Lord Byron, Chap. IV) analyses its influence on Manfred, and Byron himself points out his verbal dependence in his notes to lines 645-650 of Siege of Corinth (1815). For a pantheistic concept of religious worship strongly reminiscent of Vathek, see Letters, II, 366 (1813); cf. Letters, II, 151 (1812).

[11]Childe Harold, i, st. 15 (1812). Sarrazin points out the resemblance and notes considerable dependence elsewhere upon Castle of Indolence, in Englische Studien, XVI, 462 ff.

[12]Manfred Eimer's Byron und der Kosmos is necessary to any detailed study of this field. The present account avails itself of much of his work without separate acknowledgements, and also incorporates some parts of J. O.. E. Donner's Lord Byrons Weltanschauung; even though their conclusions are not entirely accepted, their data are indispensable.

refracting telescopes.[13] Astronomical advance was being
paralleled by the extension of geological investigations.
Buffon's theory that during former geologic ages organic life
had undergone successive transformations, further developed
by Erasmus Darwin and Lamarck, was the prototype of modern
accounts of evolution. Palaeontologists wondered about the
development or degeneration of organisms in terms not antici-
pated by religious revelation. Cuvier's theories, that the
earth had been created of the wreckage of earlier worlds de-
stroyed in hypothetical cataclysms, seemed to shed new light
upon Lucretius' belief in the imperishability of matter, as
well as upon the scriptural stories of creation and deluge
and the discoveries of fossil remains. No man with Byron's
interests could have remained indifferent to such thought,
for it affected him either as believer or skeptic. Scientific
discovery might supply a new revelation, or at least provide
a criticism of the old, of such a nature as would ease his inner torment between belief and doubt; although such a solution
of his inner strife was not vouchsafed him, scientific interests did occupy his busy thoughts, and often provided the
framework of later poetry.[14]

It was not, of course, with a scientific spirit as we
understand the term, but with an imaginative spirit that
Byron viewed the infinity about him. This spirit is traceable in his earliest poems,[15] and it is noteworthy that in
later years, either in his reminiscences or in retrospective
poetry of autobiographical significance, he frequently testi-
fied to the power which the heavens exert upon an imaginative
spirit.[16] In an outwardly Christian lyric, When Coldness
Wraps this Suffering Clay (1815), he mingles with traditional
ideas a peculiar notion of a magnetic attraction exercised by
the stars.

One other circumstance predisposing Byron toward a
naturalistic interpretation of the world came not from books

[13]From Letters, III, 408 (1814); cf. Letters, V, 458 (1821): 'The
Night is also a religious concern; and even more so, when I viewed the
Moon and Stars through Herschell's [sic] telescope, and saw that they were
worlds.'

[14]Byron's interest in such matters seems to have been engaged by 1813,
if we may trust his reference to the megalonyx (Letters, II, 363) or to
Buffon (Letters, II, 368). The Translation from Horace (1807) displays
'an expiring world,' but probably indicates little of permanent importance.
See also the original text of Hints from Horace, Poetical Works, I, 390,
note 1.

[15]See Ossian's Address to the Sun in 'Carthon' (1805); A Version of
Ossian's Address to the Sun (1806); and Curse of Minerva, vv. 1-18 (1811).

[16]See the description of a night in the Troad, Letters, III, 241 (1815);
Siege of Corinth, vv. 242-251 (1815); in particular Manfred, II.ii.156-169;
op. cit. III.iv.261-305 (1817); and his humorous treatment of the theme in
Don Juan, i, st. 92-93 (1818).

but from personal experience. A normal boyish delight in natural scenery, even though recorded in poems so insipid in
treatment as scarcely to merit serious attention,[17] provided
him a ready means of escape from social intercourse with other
persons, both in boyhood, when his lameness and hereditary
shyness made such intercourse a source of nervous tension,
and in later years, when his own conduct had necessitated
exile from England. Hence the famous stanzas of Childe Harold
in which love of nature and social isolation are inextricably
intermingled:

> Where rose the mountains, there to him were friends;
> Where roll'd the ocean, thereon was his home;
> Where a blue sky, and flowing clime, extend,
> He had the passion and the power to roam;
> The desert, forest, cavern, breaker's foam,
> Were unto him companionship; they spake
> A mutual language, clearer than the tome
> Of his land's tongue, which he would oft forsake
> For Nature's pages glass'd by sunbeams on the lake.
>   Childe Harold, iii, st. 13 (1816).

Thrown thus upon nature to find what substitute he
could for the human relationships disrupted by the exile, he
was prompted to seek in nature a quality akin to personality.
Childe Harold displays not mere natural description but the
definite avowal of imaginative experience. Hence his letter
to Augusta: 'I have lately repeopled my mind with Nature.'[18]
In this frame of mind, the old argument from design
as an evidence of the divine plan, though earlier found in
Young, will find frequent repetition. He hails the scenery of
Switzerland as 'wonder-works of God and Nature's hand,' 'a
work divine.'[19]
From these manifold influences arises Byron's naturalism in religious thought; although naturalism seems to exclude
the supernatural, and to attempt the explanation of the world

[17]See The Adieu, st. 3 and 6 (1807); Lachin Y Gair (1807); When I Roved
a Young Highlander, st. 1 and 4 (1808); I Would I Were a Careless Child,
st. 1, 2, and 7 (1808); Childe Harold, ii, st. 37 (1812); and (in retro-
spect) The Island, ii, vv. 284-297 and note thereto.
[18]Letters, III, 355 (1816); there are many such instances in which nature replaces man, anticipating the poetic animism which was shortly to
appear. See Childe Harold, iii, st. 5: 'shapes which dwell. . . .in the
soul's haunted cell' (1816); Childe Harold, iii, st. 68: 'Lake Leman woos
me' (1816); The Dream, vv. 105-125, 195-201 (1816); Manfred, II.ii.156-
173: 'My joy was in the Wilderness' (1816); Epistle to Augusta, vv. 81-
88: 'Nature. . . :was my early friend, and now shall be my sister.'
(1816).
[19]Childe Harold, iii, st. 10, 46, and 109 (1816).

by means of impersonal laws and agencies, it is not antithetical to the spirit of reverence and devotion wnich in-
forms traditional Christianity. Byron's repeated denials of
irreligion can here be reconciled with evidences of skepticism: the declaration that he was not an atheist show that he
recognized his conformity to certain aspects of religious
thought current among his first masters. Only when naturalism
rejects specific dogma such as special creation or the fixity
of species, that is, dogmas which its method does not support or
which they even contravene, is it reflected in Byron as
skepticism. And occasionally Byron was inclined to treat divine agency and the operations of nature as though they were
one, and thus to approach an attitude which finds God immanent
in all things. Such a tendency looks toward pantheism, and
in 1816 Shelley was at hand to intensify and to clarify Byron's
speculations so that his poetry was transformed. Before that
time, however, the reflection of his tumultuous experience
took the form which poetic tradition provided.

II

THE MEETING WITH SHELLEY

The vast improvement in Byron's poetry during the summer of 1816 repudiates no earlier interest. New but related
types of speculation take their places beside the old without
displacing them. There appear three new themes: declarations
that the objects of the physical world are animate; the belief
that man is substantially an attribute of the same being which
is manifested in his physical surroundings and at death re-
sumes union with it; and the exaltation of love as a unifying
and articulate principle. In the third canto of Childe Harold,
written when exile was inducing intense reflection and demand-
ing vigorous pursuit of new interests, written furthermore
within sound of the voice of a great poetic companion, these
themes emerge so suddenly and so intensely as to constitute a
new period for Byron's poetry.[20]

The first two of these themes, that common objects are
animate, and that men and things are both attributes of God,
are what we might expect of a poet who had recently discovered
theories of being which conceive of ideas and things, that is,
thought and extension, as the parallel and intimately corre-
lated attributes of a single universal substance. Such theories would place Byron's thought upon a monistic basis, if we

[20]Heinrich Gillardon's Shelleys Einwirkung auf Byron and Eimer's Lord
Byron und der Kosmos both deal with this period in greater detail than is
necessary here. They first compiled much information, incorporated into
this chapter and used without detailed acknowledgment wherever useful.
Richter's account of the significance of Shelley's friendship is excellent
(Lord Byron, p. 264 ff.).

could be certain that he had mastered or at least read
Spinoza, which is far from certain. Byron never explicitly
stated such a principle, and we lack irrefutable proof that he
ever heard it enunciated. One cannot, however, escape the
conviction that he might easily learn something of Spinoza
from Shelley at second hand, and very likely did; he could
moreover have been influenced by Shelley himself. Lucretius
and Pope are most certainly to be taken into account. It
should not be overlooked, however, that Byron's monism is implicit, never explicit; he was fundamentally a dualist, and
poetry born of this notion is a temporary concern.[21]

    The influence of Shelley's style rather than Byron's
poetic animism may account for his beginning to use such
phrases as 'Spirit of the Universe,' 'Genius of the place,'
or 'the Spirit of each spot.'[22] And during this period, the
suggestion of Shelley or the recent acquaintance with Goethe's
Faust may account for the personification of natural phenomena
for purposes of dramatic representation in Manfred.[23] But in
bolder style Byron asserts (speaking of Roman ruins) that

> There is given
> Unto the things of earth, which Time hath bent,
> A spirit's feeling.
> > Childe Harold, iv, st. 129 (1818).

More fancifully, he suggests:

> The mind can make
> Substance, and people planets of its own.
> > The Dream, vv. 19-20 (1816).[24]

Pope's Essay on Man also played its part in winning

---

[21]Byron rather frequently indicates his familiarity with atomistic
theories, commonplaces of the day, and not exclusively the teachings of
writers just named. See Manfred, I.ii.370, or II.i.55 (1816). Byron
dwells frequently upon chaos as the origin and goal of existence, the
'womb of nature and perhaps her grave'; in this connection see Prophecy
of Dante, ii, 41-45 (1819); Childe Harold, iv, st. 54, v. 6 (1818). Often
he speculates about the being of celestial bodies: Manfred, III.ii.181
(1817); op. cit., I.1.110 ff.; Don Juan, 1, st. 92 (1818); Prophecy of
Dante, iii, 9 (1819). See also, for his interest in the destruction of
heavenly bodies, Manfred, I.i.42 ff.; op. cit., II.iv.382 (1816); and
Childe Harold, iv, st. 46 (1818).

[22]See The Dream, v. 196 (1816); Childe Harold, iii, st. 74; op. cit.,
iii, st. 109 (1816); op. cit., iv, st. 68, 177 (1818). Richter maintains
that Byron was at this period feeling his way into Shelley's world of ap-
paritions (Lord Byron, p. 264 ff.).

[23]Matthew Gregory Lewis translated Faust orally while he and Byron
were at Coligny together in 1816; see Letters, V, 36-37.

[24]Compare with these Childe Harold, iii, st. 6: 'to create, and in

Byron temporarily to a monistic point of view. Pope had maintained in the Essay that all existence is but a part of the
whole; [25] Byron was perfectly familiar with this poem before
1816, and only Shelley's stimulation was necessary to make him
employ the theme:

> From the high host
> Of stars to the lull'd lake and mountain-coast,
> All is concentred in a life intense,
> Where not a beam nor air nor leaf is lost,
> But hath a part of being, and a sense
> Of that which is of all Creator and defence.
>   Childe Harold, iii, st. 89 (1816). [26]

The second of Byron's new ideas, that death is but a
reunion with 'the whole,' complicates a statement made earlier,
that from a Christian assurance of immortality entertained during boyhood, his skepticism prompted him more and more to see
death as annihilation. This idea in turn was submerged, and
under the influence of his newly found interests he began to
suspect that death, while not a survival of an individual personality, was a fusion or reunion of the soul with a diffuse
and imperishable fund of being (his wording is always vague).
This is analogous to his Lucretian notion of the imperishability of matter when it is viewed from the atomist's point of
view. The influence of Lucretius became stronger in these
years, and his formulas of expression show this rather definitely. [27] Byron does not hint, of course, that the restoration

---

creating live. . . .we endow With form our fancy' (1816); loc. cit., st.
14: 'he could watch the stars, till he had peopled them with beings'
(1816); Manfred, II.ii.183: 'the peopled infinite' (1816); Childe Harold,
iv, st. 5-6: 'beings of the mind. . . .things whose strong reality outshines our fairyland' (1818).

[25]Essay on Man, particularly Book I, vv. 267-276, Book III, vv. 17-23.

[26]Cf. Childe Harold, iii, 72: 'I become portion of that around me';
loc. cit., st. 73: 'I am absorb'd, and this is life'; loc. cit., st. 75:
'mountains, waves, and skies, a part of me'; loc. cit., st. 90, 'truth,
which through our being then doth melt'; loc. cit., st. 96: 'night, and
clouds, and thunder, and a soul to make these felt and feeling'; op. cit.,
iv, st. 178: 'To mingle with the universe'; Epistle to Augusta, v. 84:
'mingle with the quiet of her sky.'

[27]He believes, for instance, that the sum of things is being constantly
renewed. See Childe Harold, iii, st. 74 (1816); cf. op. cit., iv, st. 151:
'replenishing its source with life, as our freed souls rejoin the universe'
(1818). Hence Childe Harold, iii, st. 90: 'The spectre Death, had he sub-
stantial power to harm,' i.e., death is not harmful to substance. Cf. Don
Juan, iii, st. 104 (1819); and Marino Faliero, V. iii. 722-725:

of the individual to the universal is a mechanistic process
identical with the mutability of matter, but only an analogy
to it:

> What is this Death?--a quiet of the heart?
> The whole of that of which we are a part?
> For life is but a vision. . . .
>   The under-earth inhabitants--are they
> But mingled millions decomposed to clay?. . .
> Or have they their own language? and a sense
> Of breathless being--darkened and intense
> As midnight in her solitude?
>
> Fragment (1816)

One of course recognizes in such phrases as 'the things mis-
named Death and existence'[28] or the notion that the dead have
their own language the influence of ideas which Shelley was
later to employ in Prometheus Unbound.
       Less far-reaching in its effects upon Byron's later
thought is the deification of love in Childe Harold. The
sources are not far to seek. Byron's acquaintance with Pope
would have familiarized him with a conception of love
grounded upon the unity of all being. This is the kernel of
Pope's ethics; love is an active principle manifesting itself
in ethical conduct among men and in the justice of God. 'Whatever is, is right.' Man is imperfect in the sense that he is
incomplete, a link in a perfect chain which shadows forth the
infallible and eternal ordering of the universe by a 'first
cause.'[29] But Byron has also an indirect indebtedness to Pope
through Rousseau; he adopted from Rousseau a conception of
Love which the latter had already found in Pope. Rousseau is
the immediate influence upon Byron's pantheism of love, and
Pope is a prototype of both.[30]

> I speak to Time, and to Eternity
> Of which I grow a portion, not to man.
> Ye elements! in which to be resolved
> I hasten. . . .

[28]The Dream, vv. 2-5 (1816). Richter explains Byron's changing ideas
about death during this period entirely as a result of Shelley's influence
(Lord Byron, p. 266 ff.).

[29]Essay on Man, Book iii, vv. 207-209, 235, 508-509; Book iv, 357-540.

[30]See Rousseau's reference to Pope in Nouvelle Héloïse, Partie II,
Lettre XVIII. See Byron's note to Childe Harold, iii, st. 99: 'love in
its most extended and sublime capacity. . . .is the great principle of the
universe. . . .of which, though knowing ourselves a part, we lose our individuality, and mingle in the beauty of the whole. If Rousseau had never
written, nor lived, the same associations would not less have belonged to
such scenes.' Byron quotes freely from Rousseau, both from the Héloïse
and Les Confessions, in the notes to the familiar stanzas of Childe Harold,

The new poetry of love does not represent a sudden
access of new beliefs, nor a Weltanschauung won by dint of
persevering application to any body of speculation. It is
rather an adventitious use of material which had lain unem-
ployed; its appearance is to be explained as the effect of
travel in the regions made famous by Rousseau. Were it not
the product of a transient suggestion, it would appear more
frequently afterward, but the fact is that he seldom expressed such ideas again. Such stanzas are, in a word,
Byron's typical occasional poetry. At Cadiz he wrote of bull-
fights; at Clarens he wrote of love.

There is also evident during the second period the
further development of that nature-mysticism which before
1816 had appeared in a form similar to the poetry of natural
religion. It was a realm in which Wordsworth might easily influence him. The tendency to narrate his own poetic development with relation to nature, as in The Dream, Manfred, and
the third canto of Childe Harold, is reminiscent of The Ex-
cursion, Tintern Abbey, and indeed of Shelley's Alastor and
Young's Night Thoughts. The specific influences of Wordsworth are rather well known. [31]

The continued influence of the tradition of Young is
to be expected of a mind which grows by accretion rather than
by selection. Just as the poetry of natural religion provided an easy access to purely pantheistic beliefs, so it
continued parallel to those beliefs. The naturalistic mode
of worship and the pantheistic concept of the unity of all being are now placed side by side:

> My altars are the mountains and the ocean,
> Earth, air, stars,--all that springs from the
> great Whole,
> Who hath produced, and will receive the soul.
> Don Juan, iii, st. 104 (1819) [32]

---

iii, st. 81, 94-104. Cf. Giaour, vv. 1131-1140 (1813). For more detailed
treatment see also Otto Schmidt, Rousseau und Byron. Byron may have received some stimulation from Erasmus Darwin's Temple of Nature, with which
Shelley probably (not certainly) familiarized him. Buffon's Histoire
Naturelle, which Byron had read at latest by 1821, is another possible
analogue (see Letters, V, 572).

[31]Such parallels as Byron's "To mingle with the quiet of her sky"
(Epistle to Augusta, v. 84) and Wordsworth's "connect The landscape with
the quiet of the sky" (Tintern Abbey, vv. 7-8) do not leave much question.
See Gillardon, Kapitel II, for the evidences of Wordsworth's influence.
Byron told Medwin, "Shelley. . . .used to dose me with Wordsworth physic
even to nausea" (Medwin, p. 135).

[32]Evidence of the continued influence of the Young-Pope-Rousseau
heritage after the meeting with Shelley appears in such lines as Childe
Harold, iii, st. 91 (1816): 'Nature's realms of worship, earth and air';

Other distinguishing marks of his earlier years con-
tinue in evidence throughout this second period. His earlier
interest in astronomy was unabated,[33] and with it the curiosity about Oriental peoples, their sun-worship, and their
legends of gigantic prehistoric races.[34]   During this time he
also manifested the impress which the theories of geologists
and palaeontologists, later to be employed in Cain, had made
upon his mind.[35]

The ferment into which Byron's mind had been thrown by
his exile and his meeting with Shelley thus establishes a second period for his work. Seeking in the prose and verse of
this period the expression of his psychological state rather
than his intellectual pursuits, one perceives that he was
prompted by ruffled feelings to seek from nature a sympathetic
communion with which his religious and philosophical thoughts
were inextricably entwined. His intellectual development was
profitable; but his emotional turmoil shows less permanent
gain from the sojourn in Switzerland. The mountains appeared
to lend sympathy, but it remained for Italy to confer sufficient composure of spirit for him to attain to a sense of
humor which, mocking and cynical though it may be, is very
nearly the gauge of his ultimate sanity. He does occasionally testify that Alpine scenery has had a restorative effect
upon his spirits.[36]   Manfred, furthermore, seems to show a
temporary power to defy the consequences of guilt. Perhaps
poems like Darkness arise from a momentary reconciliation of
scientific theories of cosmogony with Biblical revelation.
Byron profited in part by speculations which permitted him at
times to look forward to immortality, and which taught that
the end of an individual existence is of no importance to the
universal substance. His earlier threats to leave off writing[37] were hence not carried out, because new interests
brought fresh inspiration. He seemed to be approaching a new
outlook upon the universe and man's relation to it. But

Childe Harold, iv, st. 183 (1818): 'mirror, where the Almighty's form
glasses itself in tempests.'

[33]See Marino Faliero, II.i.396-398 (1820); Don Juan, iv, st. 56 (1819);
Don Juan, v, st. 144-145 (1820); op. cit., v, st. 109 (1820); Monody on
the Death of Sheridan, vv. 25-36, 57-58 (1816); Mazeppa, vv. 648-652
(1818-1819).

[34]Manfred, III.ii.174-201 (1817).

[35]Manfred, I.i.68 ff.; op. cit., I.ii.353-361; Don Juan, iv, st. 33
(1819).

[36]He seeks to 'remount. . . .with a fresh pinion' (Childe Harold, iii,
st. 73); he resolves that 'in me shall loneliness renew thoughts hid, but
not less cherish'd'; he will 'aak of Nature that with which she will
comply' (Epistle to Augusta, st. 11). But we read at one moment, 'I am
content' (op. cit., st. 15), and at another, 'I feel an ebb in my philosophy' (ibid., st. 9).

[37]See Letters, III, 201 and 274 (1815, 1816).

Byron was too volatile to sustain such a mood. Despite the
fervid lines about losing one's identity in the scenery of
Clarens and Meillerie, he wrote the next September, 'I am a
lover of Nature and an admirer of Beauty. . . .But in all
this--the recollections of bitterness. . . .have preyed upon
me here; and neither the music of the Shepherd, the crashing
of the Avalanche, nor the torrent, the mountain, the Glacier,
the Forest, nor the Cloud, have for one moment lightened the
weight upon my heart, nor enabled me to lose my own wretched
identity in the majesty, and the power, and the glory,
around, above, and beneath me.'[38]   The hope of forgetting himself in nature was elusive, and after that summer in Switzerland he never referred to the idea again until almost the end
of his life.[39]

III

ITALY

    An earlier chapter has indicated that a period of
more mature thought is marked by productions like Cain and
Don Juan. It is not distinguished from the earlier years by
any resignation to the conditions imposed by mortal nature.
It is rather a period in which the affectations of Harold and
the heroics of Manfred are dropped for bitter irony and mocking laughter. For the investigation of Byron's naturalism
somewhat the same division is required. With Cain,
Sardanapalus, and the resumption of Don Juan the following
year, the poetry of pure pantheism is left behind.
    Byron's mature years show a passionate love of the
heavens such as his earlier poetry seldom equalled. Cain and
Sardanapalus, particularly the beginning of the fifth act of
the latter, bear witness to this. 'I am always most religious
upon a sunshiny day; as if there was some association between
an internal approach to greater light and purity, and the
kindler of this dark lanthorn of our external existence.'[40]
So he had written long before the exile. Now he habitually
employs an idiom in which constellations, the zodiac, the
milky way, comets, meteors, and spheres become familiar terms.
What had been nebulous in his earlier poetry is now definite;
his thought is surcharged with the adoration of the heavens
and of infinite space:

    [38]Letters, III, 564 (1816). Cf. ibid., 560: 'Passed whole woods of
withered pines, all withered; trunks stripped and barkless, branches
lifeless; done by a single winter,--their appearance reminded me of me
and my family.'
    [39]The Island, ii, vv. 586-593 (1823).
    [40]Letters, III, 408 (1814); cf. Blessington, pp. 90-91 (1823).

The symbols
Of the Invisible are the loveliest
Of what is visible.
Cain, I.1.496-498 (1821).

He abandons for the most part traditional imagery, and adopts
as his data the theories of Fontenelle and the discoveries of
Herschel. What may at first sight appear to be pure fantasy
in Cain, The Vision of Judgment, and Heaven and Earth shows
upon closer examination that science has tended to supplant
tradition. The cosmology of these poems is Byron's deliberate
intent to infuse into his poetry a scientific verisimilitude.
'Metaphysics open a vast field; Nature and the anti-Mosaical
speculation of the origin of the world, a wide range, and
sources of poetry that are shut out by Christianity.'[41] From
the cataclysmic theories of Cuvier and the atomists' teachings
that all being is a state of ceaseless activity and transfor-
mation, he infers a universal principle at work in the world
which creates from the fragments of old celestial bodies new
ones manifesting all degrees of change from the nature of the
predecessors. 'Oh, world! which was and is, what is cosmogony?'[42] A theory that other planets might also be populated
had already been advanced by Fontenelle. What germs of truth
might not be contained in the old Chaldaean belief that great
rulers had been apotheosized as stars, or in the Book of Enoch
with its teaching that planets are guided by angels? Medwin
tells us that he had begun to suspect that myth and fable
might shadow forth 'dim images of the past.'[43] A mingling of
all these interests into a fairly consistent set of ideas pro-
duced the philosophical background of Cain and the narrative
framework of Heaven and Earth.[44]

These speculations were also applied to human life.
He was alert to the idea that organic life was subject to mu-
tations; more specifically, he suspected that it tended to
degenerate. Hence, men and animals of the present world are
the imperfect representatives of more glorious prototypes.[45]
The gigantic prehistoric (i.e., pre-Adamite) forms are represented by such palaeontological remains as those of the

[41]Medwin, p. 47 (1821-2).

[42]Don Juan, ix, st. 20 (1822).

[43]Medwin, p. 129.

[44]See also Letters, V, 162 (1821); Don Juan, ix, st. 13, st. 37 ff.
(1822); op. cit., xv, st. 99 (1823). The ideas are humorously treated in
Vision of Judgment, st. 16.

[45]Deformed Transformed, III. i. 58-61 (1822); Heaven and Earth, I.iii.
394-410 (1822); Don Juan, ix, st. 46 (1822); Buffon had formerly proposed
the theory that the Patagonians of South America were the survivors of gigantic prehistoric races. See also the Preface of Cain, and Letters, V,
368 (1821).

mammoth.[46]   Here, in the objective and impersonal conclusions
of other men, he could feed his own scorn of the men and
things of this puny world.

Byron was by no means a leader in the thought of the
nineteenth century, but his poetry contains much that is
symptomatic of the culture about him. We have in Byron the
anticipation of evolutionary thought: species have not been
fixed since all eternity. More and more he was coming to pin
his faith in science, not in tradition. 'I suppose we shall
soon travel by air-vessels; make air instead of sea-voyages
. . . .Where shall we set bounds to the power of steam?. . . .
We are at present in the infancy of science.'[47] Here speaks a
modern mind.

In the poetry of Byron's final period he tried, with
small success, to clarify his conceptions of the soul and of
death. Although Byron's speculations about the nature of being are extremely difficult to reduce to formal definitions,
largely because his own ideas were hazy, it would be fair to
say that they are primarily reflections of his belief in the
continuity of existence. Having the scientist's faith in the
imperishability of matter, he retains the traditional
Lucretian belief that all forms of being manifest ceaseless
disintegration and re-creation. But the constant transforma-
tion of the forms of nature is determined by 'fixed necessity'--in reality a sovereign will operating in accordance
with a divine plan which reflects the power of the Creator.
Just as Byron's skeptic reflection tended to doubt that truth
was static, so his natural philosophy emphasized the dynamic
nature of being:

                    From the star
     To the winding worm, all life is motion; and
     In life, commotion is the extremest point
     Of life. The planet wheels till it becomes
     A comet, and destroying as it sweeps
     The stars, goes out. The poor worm winds its way,
     Living upon the death of other things,
     But still, like them, must live and die, the subject
     Of something which has made it live and die.
     You must obey what all obey, the rule
     Of fix'd necessity.
                    Deformed Transformed, I.1.590-600.

The principle of the imperishability of being was so well
grounded in his thought that from it he inferred some idea of

---

[46]These and similar speculations are component parts of Cain, II.ii.
337-352; Don Juan, viii, st. 137 (1822); op. cit., ix, st. 38 (1822);
Deformed Transformed, I.1.304; op. cit., III.i.50-61 (1822).

[47]Medwin, pp. 129-130. Cf. Don Juan, x, st. 2 (1822).

a future immortality. This was, of course, inconsistent with
his skeptical denial of the possibility of attaining such
knowledge, and was, like his skepticism, an intermittent mood.
But Byron was not a systematic thinker. Once the idea of immortality had been ushered in by his temporary inclination toward monism, he was likely to recur to it at any time. The
expression of such belief in his poetry is often vague and con-
fusing; an interpretation of his lines demands that we hazard
a highly subjective estimate of the degree to which lines
placed in the mouths of his dramatic characters may fairly be
said to indicate his own beliefs; and one is dismayed to find
his statements displaying manifold gradations from a rationalistic concern with the means of knowing to a purely mystic assurance akin to that of Christianity.[48] He clings with particular tenacity to the notion that death and life are 'mis-
named,' not properly to be understood as contradictory terms
like being and extinction, but different forms of existence.[49]
They are not realities but appearances; hence he appears to
blend the semipantheist's belief in the continuity of being
and the skeptic's suspicion that the reports of human understanding are not final:

> Between two worlds life hovers like a star,
> 'Twixt night and morn, upon the horizon's verge.
> How little do we know that which we are!
> How less what we may be! The eternal surge
> Of time and tide rolls on, and bears afar
> Our bubbles; as the old burst, new emerge,
> Lash'd from the foam of ages; while the graves
> Of empire heave but like some passing waves.
> Don Juan, xv, st. 99 (1823)[50]

To turn for the moment from inferences drawn from
Byron's poetry, there is in his 'Detached Thoughts' a prose
statement of his credo: 'Of the Immortality of the Soul, it
appears to me that there can be little doubt, if we attend for
a moment to the action of the Mind. It is in perpetual activity. I used to doubt of it, but reflection has taught me
better. It acts also so very independent of body. . . .Now,
that this should not act separately as well as jointly, who
can pronounce?. . . .How far our future life will be individual, or, rather, how far it will at all resemble our
present existence, is another question; but that the Mind is

[48]Cf. Letters, VI, 50, note 2; and Heaven and Earth, I.i.110-125.
[49]These somewhat Shelleyan notions begin as early as 1816 in The Dream,
vv. 2-5, and have been observed earlier in the chapter; but they persist
in Cain, I.i.105, and may be observed again in Blessington's accounts of
his conversations (p. 150 and p. 507) in 1823.
[50]Cf. Don Juan, xv, st. 2.

eternal, seems as probable as that the body is not so.[51]

One element in Byron's thought remains constant throughout all his work, whether it be cast in a skeptic mood or in one which seeks through natural phenomena to lighten the burden of the mystery. 'How, raising our eyes to heaven, or directing them to the earth, can we doubt of the existence of God?--or how, turning them to what is within us, can we doubt that there is something within us more noble and more durable than the clay of which we are formed? Those who do not hear, or are unwilling to listen to those feelings, must necessarily be of a vile nature.'[52] No one formula describing his conception of Deity will be found universally applicable to all his poetry. In some instances, when he feels most strongly an immediate divine agency spiritually present in the operations and objects of nature, it seems that his God is immanent in the manner of the pantheist's thought. More frequently, writing in the manner of Pope or Young, he sees the world as an intricate wonder which implies a Creator otherwise assumed to transcend His creation. Since Christianity loosely embraces both these conceptions, he was never required to reconcile them. But he seems never to have thought about the question. The latter of these two conceptions, that of a transcendent Deity, is, however, his most characteristic one; he seemed to feel the immanence of God only during the reveries of natural piety prompted by the scenery of Switzerland.

The course of Byron's speculations about the natural order presents the complexities which are to be expected in poetry written during a transitional period of the history of thought. He stands midway between the past and the problems which were to concern the nineteenth century. His earliest period, as might be expected, is the one which most clearly marks his relation to tradition. The middle period represents the ferment of ideas attendant upon the attainment of greater stature. The ripening of his powers in Italy brought about the most marked expressions of his naturalism, but is distinguished by vigorous attention to contemporary scientific theory rather than by the immediate stimulation of persons and scenes.

Except for the period during which the influence of Shelley's thought and personality excited Byron's interest in systematic monism, he was never a thorough-going pantheist in the sense of one who feels convinced of the unity of all being. Byron's poetry before his stay in Switzerland and afterward shows that his point of view was habitually dualistic. He always treated mind and matter, soul and body, spirit and clay, as though they were mutually exclusive concepts.

[51]Letters, V, 456-457 (1821).
[52]Kennedy, Conversations, p. 577; Gamba dates this about 1820.

> Think not
> The earth, which is thine outward cov'ring, is
> Existence--it will cease, and thou wilt be
> No less than thou art now.
>
> Cain, I.i.116-120 [53]

It is indeed true that he adopted the Lucretian belief in the
continuity of substance, and that in characteristic recurrent
moods he believed that the soul would rejoin at death the
whole of which it was a part. 'Matter is eternal, always
changing, but reproduced, and, as far as we can comprehend
Eternity, Eternal; and why not Mind? Why should not the Mind
act with and upon the universe? as portions of it act upon
and with the congregated dust called Mankind?' [54] But note
that he inferred the unity of 'mind' (as distinguished from
'portions of it') from the imperishability of matter, and not
from the metaphysical doctrine that thought, like extension,
is the attribute of one substance. Byron was not a systematic metaphysician; his hold upon the subtleties of
ontological theory was at best precarious. He was not likely, therefore, to be won over to pantheism by the cogency of
logic, but rather by an imaginative poetic act. Although not
wholly unacquainted with the logical processes of pantheistic
speculation, he attained his temporary assurance of the unity
of being by way of aesthetic excitation as well as by rationalistic process. It is noteworthy that except for the
notes to the last two cantos of Childe Harold, evidences of
pure pantheism are confined almost exclusively to his poetry.
He was a monist or mystic only in poetic feeling; his prose
shows rather the characteristic inclination to see in nature
a manifestation of the divine plan. The idea of unity represented to him a feeling which he had experienced; and when
the conditions which induced that experience were no longer
at hand, the rationalistic support was not sufficiently har-
monious to his own nature to sustain a consistent monism.
After 1817 his pantheism was no longer pure or active. Although he had no naive faith in the testimony of the senses,
as his trend toward subjective idealism attests, he was still
too much of a realist to feel any abiding certainty of the
unity of thought and extension. 'I have often been inclined
to Materialism in philosophy but could never bear its intro-
duction into Christianity, which appears to me essentially

---

[53]Cf. Devil's Drive, vv. 221 ff. (1813); Childe Harold, iii, st. 14
(1816); Manfred, I.i.156-163 (1816); Letters, IV, 102 (1817); Sardanapalus,
V.i.159-160, 422-424 (1821); Cain, II.i.164 (1821); Letters, V, 211 (1821);
loc. cit., 456 ff., 'Detached Thoughts' nos. 96, 97, 98 (1821); Deformed
Transformed, I.i passim (1822); Blessington, p. 90 ff., 307-308 (1823).

[54]Letters, V, 458 (1821).

founded upon the Soul.'[55] Which is to say that matter and
soul are different entities, to be investigated by different
types of thought. His mind was predisposed to dualistic cate-
gories.

The religious speculation of the eighteenth century
emphasized the 'natural' (i.e., not the 'revealed') evidences
of the Divine Nature; it had too much in common both with
Deism and with Christianity to reach the Spinozistic formula
of Deus sive Natura. Byron's most characteristic conception
of the Divine hence retains the idea of a transcendent Deity,
sovereign, manifested in his works, but not identified with
them. He stands here with Pope, not with the Spinozists.
There is no holy passion for natura naturans; Byron retains
only the belief that substance is imperishable, and this is
inferred, not from metaphysics, but from the conclusions of
science in astronomy, geology, and biology. This is Byron's
modernity; he reflects the speculative thought of his own
times, not, like Shelley, the philosophy of earlier days. His
interests were in the living present as well as in the past;
when he turned to history it was in search of that which had
been experienced rather than that which had been thought. He
sought an understanding of existent reality, and challenged
traditional belief whenever it conflicted with new-found
truth.

Byron's break with traditionalism manifested itself
both in his skepticism and in his naturalism. The skeptic
element was the negative or the enabling factor which left
him free for untrammelled consideration of the implications of
scientific discovery; his naturalism was on the other hand
positivistic. His skepticism, with its alert attention to
theories of idealism and developmental truth, was concerned
with the problem of knowledge; his naturalism led him to the
problem of being. His skeptic attitude toward supernatural-
ism reinforced his tendency toward naturalistic thought.
These are the devious paths of his mind, the habitual grooves
of his thought. They led to no synthesis, they attained no
unique truth; but through them ran a current of poetry which
will always challenge investigation.

[55]Letters, V, 458 (1821).

Chapter Four

ROMAN CATHOLICISM

A glorious remnant of the Gothic pile
  (While yet the church was Rome's) stood half apart
In a grand arch, which once screen'd many an aisle.
  These last had disappear'd--a loss to art:
The first yet frown'd superbly o'er the soil,
  And kindled feelings in the roughest heart,
Which mourn'd the power of time's or tempest's march,
In gazing on that venerable arch.
Don Juan, xiii, st. 59.

If the classical element n Byron's poetry, defined by
an eminent editor as 'a certain predominance of the intellect
over the emotions, and a reliance on broad effects rather than
on subtle impressions,'[1] may be said to manifest itself in his
reflective poetry as rationalism, the romantic aspects of his
genius are partly to be traced to his frequent surrender to

        things whose strong realit,
Outshines our fairy-land: in shape and hues
More beautiful than our fantastic sky
. . . .
They came like truth, and disappear'd like dreams.

The classical element has been further traced in
Byron's use of 'form and action in his representation of nature.'[2] If the touchstone of romanticism be 'the blending,
iridescent light' of some of Byron's contemporaries, then it
was the romantic artist in Byron who wrote of the great
window at Newstead:

A mighty window, hollow in the centre,
  Shorn of its glass of thousand colourings,
Through which the deepen'd glories once could enter,
  Streaming from off the sun-like seraph's wings,
Now yawns all desolate: now loud, now fainter,
  The gale sweeps through its fretwork, and oft sings
The owl his anthem, where the silenced quire
Lie with their hallelujahs quench'd like fire.
Don Juan, xiii, st. 62 (1823).

---

[1]Mr. Paul Elmer More, 'The Wholesome Revival of Byron,' p. 801.
[2]Op. cit., p. 806: '. . . .there is little of the blending iridescent
light of romance. . . .and in general Byron dwells on form and action in

To press the analogy a bit further, Byron's skepticism, naturally aligning itself with eighteenth-century literature, is a manifestation of 'the predominance of intellect'; but in his imaginative sympathy with Roman Catholicism, Byron departs from classicism. In the suspension of the intellective faculties, during which he accepts the guidance of 'subtle suggestion,' there emerges his sensuous love of the concrete symbols of worship, his reverence for the storied past, and for the associations gathered about the ancestral seat of the Byrons.

Were Byron invariably a poet of intellect, he could never have left such a strange poetic record of incongruous moods. The swift alterations of temper, during which he wrote directly from the point of view of the moment, would be impossible to a Milton. Particularly difficult to reconcile with his incipient Catholicism is the harsh satire of Roman worship in his earlier poetry. It is necessary to recognize that in Byron's attacks upon Catholicism, several different motives may be traced. In that characteristic mood of criticism and negation which may be designated as skepticism, he viewed all religions as equally faulty in creed or practice. There are, however, other expressions of anti-Catholicism which appear to amount to little more than a provincial, 'no-popery' Protestantism; these, be it said, are not the product of matured thought. There is also to be distinguished the statement of orthodox Protestant principles antithetical to the Roman creed. And some note must be taken of Byron's satirical treatment of the Roman clergy in a spirit that is neither skepticism nor Protestantism, but rather a mood of banter such as might be found in writers born and bred to Catholicism.

Unthinking prejudice inherited from English Protestantism is virtually the only explanation which can be advanced for his early anti-Catholicism. That an Englishman of the days of the Regency should find in Catholic beliefs matter for jesting is not in itself significant.[3] Many of his witticisms, coarse enough in all conscience, are traditional with English Protestantism. [4] But Byron sometimes betrays an

his representation of nature, whereas his contemporaries, and notably Shelley, revel in her variety of hues.'

[3]See Letters, I, 63 (1805) for pleasantries about the doctrine of Purgatory. Cf. Childe Harold, i, st. 71 (1812):

> Thy saint adorers count the rosary.
> Much is the VIRGIN teased to shrive them free
> (Well do I ween the only virgin there)

[4]'No-popery' Protestantism is among the traits ascribed to Horace Hornem, the pseudo-author of that dreary satire The Waltz (See Note to Preface, 1813). See also phrases like 'Babylonian whore' (Childe Harold, i, st. 29, 1812) or 'our Lady of Babylon' (Waltz, v. 21, note). Cf. jests about 'Mrs. Joseph' and the 'Immaculate Riddle' (Letters, I, 122, 1812). In The Deformed Transformed (1822) Byron is represented by hunchbacked Arnold, not by Caesar; but note for traditional satire Caesar's words

insularity completely at variance with his professed cosmopolitan point of view.[5]   The crassly anti-Semitic passage
satirizing the Rothschild brothers in the Age of Bronze shows
how readily, even in later years, he could lapse into vulgar
abuse.[6]

But such instances of insularity are really few. More
often than not his spleen is occasioned by some specific circumstance, for example the desecration by clerics of spots
hallowed by literary associations.[7] More sincere in their expression, and hence more nearly valid as religious criticism,
are the occasional avowals of positive belief alien to Roman
Catholicism. 'In religion, I favour the Catholic emancipation,' he wrote, 'but do not acknowledge the Pope; and I have
refused to take the sacrament, because I do not think eating
bread or drinking wine from the hand of an earthly vicar will
make me an inheritor of heaven.'[8] It was in somewhat the same
spirit that he 'rejected and ejected three Priest-loads of
spiritual consolation by threatening to turn Mussulman if they

---

'hermaphrodite of empire' applied to Rome (I.ii.577); cf. also I.ii.612-617
for strictures against temporal power of papacy.

[5]E.g., he classes Spain with Turkey and Greece as one of 'the most
bigotted and credulous of countries' (Letters, III, 402, 1813). Cf. Letters, V, 558 (1821), Catholicism characterized as 'the most bigoted of
sects.'

[6]Byron's utter lack of critical discrimination is probably the only explanation for the recurrence of such ideas so late in life (1822-23). The
passage follows:

> (Where now, oh pope! is thy forsaken toe?
> Could it not favour Judah with some kicks?
> Or has it ceased to 'kick against the pricks?')—
> On Shylock's shore behold them stand afresh,
> To cut from nations' hearts their 'pound of flesh.'
>   Age of Bronze, vv. 699-703.

[7]Thus a note to Childe Harold, iii, st. 99, v. 5, calls the monks who
felled the Bosquet de Julie 'the miserable drones of an execrable superstition.' See also Childe Harold, iv, st. 58, on the treatment accorded
Boccaccio's tomb by the church:

>   even his tomb
> Uptorn must bear the hyaena bigot's wrong.

It should be added that Byron was readily angered by religious prejudice
whenever it received precedence above literary merit, no matter what
church was responsible: 'Of all the disgraces that attach to England in
the eye of foreigners, who admire Pope more than any of our poets. . . .
the greatest perhaps is, that there should be no place assigned to him in
Poets' Corner. . . .But he was a Catholic. . . .That accounts for his not
having any national monument. . . .The French, I am told, lock up Voltaire's tomb. Will there never be an end to this bigotry?'—Medwin,
p. 139 (1821-2).

[8]Letters, I, 173 (1808).

did not leave me in quiet.' [9] His moods of orthodox belief frequently evoked the statement that religion was properly a concern of the individual, not of any institution; he thus im-
plicitly denied the traditional claim of the Roman Church to
provide the most efficacious means by which man may enter into
relation with the divine. Thus Manfred:

> I hear thee. This is my reply: whate'er
> I may have been, or am, doth rest between
> Heaven and myself; I shall not choose a mortal
> To be my mediator.
>   Manfred, III.1.52-55.[10]

It may be noted that Byron's stern insistence upon the
immediacy of man's approach to the divine, as well as his
jests about Catholicism, are found primarily in the poetry
written before his residence in Italy. It was only in his intellectual maturity, that is, in his contact with Italian culture, that Byron learned the fine art of ecclesiastical
satire. He then began to write of church and churchmen, not
in the manner of a Bible-bred censor of human frailty, but
with that laughing mockery which is found in the literature
antecedent to the spirit of the Reformation. Jean de Meun
might have written these stanzas:

> But, ah! he died; and buried with him lay
>   The public feeling and the lawyers' fees:
> His house was sold, his servants sent away,
>   A Jew took one of his two mistresses,
>   A priest the other--at least so they say:
>   Don Juan, i, st. 34 (1818).

> The ship was evidently settling now
>   Fast by the head; and, all distinction gone,
> Some went to prayers again, and made a vow
>   Of candles to their saints--but there were none
> To pay them with; and some look'd o'er the bow;
>   Some hoisted out the boats; and there was one
> That begg'd Pedrillo for an absolution,
> Who told him to be damn'd--in his confusion.
>   Don Juan, ii, st. 44 (1818-1819).[11]

[9]This during an attack of fever at Patras in 1810. See Letters, III,
401 ff.
[10]Cf. Correspondence, I, 91 (1812): 'You talk of my "religion"; that
rests between man and his Maker. . . .'; see also Childe Harold, iv, st.
95 (1818):
> I speak not of men's creeds--they rest between
> Man and his Maker.
[11]Byron was quite aware of the part which religious satire played in

Byron did not lose his Protestant identity in the
later satire. For example, it would never occur to a Catholic
poet to explain as a special circumstance that Pedrillo died a
Catholic; it would have been taken for granted:

> He died as born, a Catholic in faith,
>   Like most in the belief in which they're bred,
> And first a little crucifix he kiss'd,
> And then held out his jugular and wrist.
>   Don Juan, ii, st. 76 (1818-1819).[12]

The change in Byron's methods of satire is paralleled
by a change of spirit in the terms of his criticism. When he
wrote in the tradition of eighteenth-century England, as in
the English Bards or in the Age of Bronze, he adopted a cen-
sorious harshness utterly different from the crisp wit of
Don Juan.[13] In his latest satire of religious establishments

---

Italian burlesque romance and of the degree of license allowed to it. See
Letters, IV, 402 (1820): 'I think my translation of Pulci will make you
stare: it must be put by the original, stanza for stanza, and verse for
verse; and you will see what was permitted in a Catholic country and a
bigotted age to a Churchman, on the score of religion:—and so tell those
buffoons who accuse me of attacking the liturgy.' See Claude M. Fuess,
Lord Byron as a Satirist in Verse, for the best available study of Byron's
relation to the tradition of verse satire in Italy and of the moral tone
he adopted from it.

[12]The same self-conscious but not hostile Protestantism occurs in Don
Juan, ii, st. 55 (1818-1819):

> All the rest perish'd; near two hundred souls
>   Had left their bodies; and what's worse, alas!
> When over Catholics the ocean rolls,
>   They must wait several weeks before a mass
> Takes off one peck of purgatorial coals,
>   Because, till people know what's come to pass,
> They won't lay out their money on the dead—
> It costs three francs for every mass that's said.

[13]Note the absence of any note of moral stricture in such lines as:

> . . . . .his majesty. . . . .
> . . . .Contrived to keep this den
> Of beauties cool as an Italian convent,
> Where all the passions have, alas! but one vent.
>
> And what is that? Devotion, doubtless—how
>   Could you ask such a question?—but we will
> Continue.
>   Don Juan, vi, st. 32-33 (1822).

Life in Italy had much to do with teaching him an easy sympathy with what

humor predominates over mere invective.

Byron's trend toward Catholicism consisted to some ex-
tent in a diminution of that denunciatory Protestantism of
which he, in common with less gifted persons, was readily
capable; and in increased use of a type of satire which, born
in Catholic cultures and practised by Catholic minds, is most
effective in realizing the intent of the satirist, the evoca-
tion, by means of laughter, of self-cognizance and self-
criticism. He abandons such cumbrous bludgeonings as The
Waltz for the swift incisions of Don Juan. The change of tone
in his poetry is of a piece with the intellectual maturity
consequent upon a widening horizon of experience. Although
his theoretical canons of literary criticism remain in essential agreement with the standards of the preceding century,
his practice is modified by contact with medievalism operating through two channels, the spirit of burlesque literary
satire, and the survival of medieval thought in the Roman
Catholicism he saw practised in Italy. Renewed interest in
points of view of medieval origin is essentially an aspect of
the romantic revival. And Byron had early been rendered receptive to that point of view by a variety of circumstances
which steadily inclined him toward Catholicism.

In a most shrewd analysis of the character of Lord
Byron, Arthur Symons makes the observation that almost every
line which Byron wrote is a reminiscence of a place or of a
passion. His poetry reflects like 'a cracked mirror' the
fragmentary and multitudinous recollections of all he had experienced.[14] The trait is clearly evidenced by Byron's strong
attachment to Newstead Abbey.

From many sources comes the testimony of the deep impression which the acquisition of land and title made upon
Byron. Indeed, no biographer seems to consider his record
complete without a rehearsal of the amusing puerilities with
which Byron received the news of his inheritance.[15] When
financial difficulties pressed upon him during the interval
between Cambridge and the first pilgrimage, on one point he
was resolute: 'Come what may, Newstead and I stand or fall
together. I have now lived on the spot, I have fixed my

Childe Harold might call 'the labyrinth of sin.' See his description of
an ecclesiastical celebration, Letters, V, 6 (1820): '. . . .there will
be a Circle, and a Faro-table. . . .The Cardinal himself is a very good-
natured little fellow, Bishop of Imola and Legate here,—a devout believer in all the doctrines of the Church. He has kept his housekeeper
these forty years, for his carnal recreation; but is reckoned a pious
man, and a moral liver.'

[14]Arthur Symons, Romantic Movement in English Poetry, p. 248.

[15]André Maurois, it will be remembered, lived at Newstead while pre-
paring his Byron; his biography hence recognizes fully the imaginative
stimulus of the surroundings.

heart upon it, and no pressure, present or future, shall in-
duce me to barter the last vestige of our inheritance. I have
that pride within me which will enable me to support difficulties. . . .I feel like a man of honour, and I will not sell
Newstead.'[16] The strength of feeling which he displayed in
connection with Newstead makes it clearly evident that a deep
sense of personal satisfaction was involved in the retention
of the Abbey. Byron's concern with the external world, with
the theatrical role he conceived his life to be, required the
éclat of a landed title.

But beyond mere egotism, there must be recognized
Byron's sincere respect for historic tradition. His veneration for the associations gathered around the Abbey was a determining influence upon his adolescence. It is unfortunate
that the attention which biographers have given to the ac-
quisitive vanity which marked Byron's feelings toward Newstead
has obscured in some measure the deeper significance which his
love for the Abbey had in developing a mind responsive to the
glamour of an historic past. For present purposes, emphasis
must be laid on the imaginative stimulus which Newstead afforded to Byron's veneration for sacred objects.

Although Byron's poetic debt to Newstead is in evidence in his earliest verse,[17] it was not until 1806 that he
recorded the impression made upon him by the specifically religious associations of the Abbey.[18] These early poems and
the reference to Newstead in the first canto of Childe Harold
comprise nearly the whole of the allusions in his early poetry
to the ecclesiastical history associated with the Abbey. The
letters, however, leave no doubt about his attachment to the
ancestral seat of the Byrons. After the exile it loomed large
in his thought as a symbol of all that he had lost;[19] the description of Newstead in the thirteenth canto of Don Juan is
vibrant with lingering regret. To him it was not mere land,
but consecrated ground; the will of Aug. 12, 1811, directed
that he be buried elsewhere for that specific reason.

From earliest youth to latest maturity Byron retained
his deep love for the Abbey. The effect of such scenes and
such memories on a wildly imaginative nature sensitive to religious feeling, superstitious, and easily awed by the supernatural, can hardly be overestimated. To the man of active
life, and particularly to one whose life is spent in strife

[16]Letters, I, 216 (1809). Byron's letters are of course utterly inconsistent on the subject. He resolved repeatedly to sell the place and
not to sell it. Once expatriated, there was no reason to retain it,
but the negotiations were not completed until 1818.

[17]'On Leaving Newstead Abbey' (1803), Fugitive Pieces.

[18]Elegy on Newstead Abbey (1806), in Poems on Various Occasions.

[19]See particularly Epistle to Augusta, vv. 72-80.

and confusion as was Byron's, the quiet seclusion of an old
abbey must have been particularly suggestive. Byron's was not
a quiet spirit, but it was a poetic spirit; what that 'haunt
of ancient peace' may have wrought upon him is evident in
Byron's sympathy for the institution of monasticism.

Lacking Shelley's satisfaction with the inner world of
the spirit, and wanting that manly poise with which Scott
viewed the external world, Byron was readily enabled to understand and sympathize with the motives which impel other spirits
to 'flee fro the presse.' Byron did not flee; but there is in
his verse a marked tendency to view monasticism as a refuge
from a world accursed. Although his earlier verse shows some
note of it,[20] the fragment Monk of Athos furnishes better evidence of the strength of the feeling; it was probably written
not far from the peak of his interest in pantheistic speculation, when one might least expect the recurrence of a mood of
Christian piety:

> Beside the confines of the Aegean main,
> Where northward Macedonia bounds the flood,
> . . . .
> With lowering port majestic Athos stands,
> Crown'd with the verdure of eternal wood,
> As yet unspoil'd by sacrilegious hands
> . . . .
> Mid scenes where Heavenly Contemplation loves
> To kindle in her soul her hallow'd fire,
> Where air and sea with rocks and woods conspire
> To breathe a sweet religious calm around,
> Weaning the thoughts from every low desire,
> And the wild waves that break with murmuring sound
> Along the rocky shore proclaim it holy ground.
>
> Sequester'd shades were Piety has given
> A quiet refuge from each earthly care,
> Whence the rapt spirit may ascend to Heaven!
> . . . .
> What bliss amidst these solitudes to share
> The happy foretaste of eternal Peace,
> Till Heaven in mercy bids your pain and sorrows cease.[21]

Although Byron was an anchorite only by way of poetic
feeling, it is interesting to note that at about the same time
that the foregoing lines were written (1816), he was making
regular visits to the Armenian monastery at St. Lazzaro, near

---

[20]Elegy on Newstead, st. 12, (1806); Giaour, vv. 971-996 (1813).

[21]Coleridge suggests that the fragment was intended for a part of the
third canto of Childe Harold. Cf. op. cit., ii, st. 27 for 'wish that
such had been his lot' (1812).

Venice, where he studied Armenian under Father Aucher. In
1819 Aucher published a grammar for English students of Armenian, printing therein Byron's translation of the Armenian
version of two epistles of Paul and the Corinthians, and his
translation of the Pleasure Houses of Byzantium. Byron had
often visited monasteries merely as routine incidents of
travel. Such was the nature of his stay at a Franciscan (he
also calls it 'Capucin') monastery in Athens. It is recounted that Byron asked permission to inhabit one of the
cells, and that he asked the father for a crucifix, which he
kissed with a great display of emotion. [22]

Byron's profound awe of the supernatural was readily
excited by such objects. Biographers have frequently called
attention to his proneness to superstition, [23] probably the
more frequently because in a man of his loud-voiced (although
intermittent) skepticism it seems incongruous. It was not
exactly gullibility that made Byron attend so closely to the
words of soothsayers. His most skeptical moments were only
alternations with those moods in which supernatural forces
seemed to him very powerful indeed. When he paid undue attention to ridiculous prophecies, he was experiencing the
acute awe of the supernatural which is evident in his attitude toward most questions of faith. As a matter of fact,
several times the predictions of soothsayers were strangely
prophetic, particularly with reference to his marriage and
his relations with Guiccioli; even less susceptible persons
might be forgiven if they were somewhat impressed.

Since Roman Catholicism makes more liberal use of
physical objects in its rites than the reformed churches,
Byron's veneration of the concrete evidences of faith was
most frequently evoked by contact with the Roman communion.
A hopelessly intolerant skeptic would not be likely to write
thus of the chalice:

> The foe came on. . . .
> And from each other's rude hands wrest
> The silver vessels saints had bless'd.
> To the high altar on they go;
> Oh, but it made a glorious show!
> On its table still behold
> The cup of consecrated gold;
> Massy and deep, a glittering prize,
> Brightly it sparkles to plunderers' eyes.

[22]Quennell (in Byron, pp. 209-210) states on the authority of a hither-
to unpublished letter that in 1814, in Byron's room in London, was a
'crucifix conspicuously hung.'

[23]E.g., Moore, Chap. IV; Galt, p. 268. Richter, p. 109, gives an account of the Oriental amulet which he carried and reproduces the script
later taken from it.

> That morn it held the holy wine
> Converted by Christ to his blood so divine.
> Siege of Corinth, vv. 986-1004 (1815).

These are admittedly not the words of the matured Byron, but even after all the mockery of Don Juan and the defiance of Cain had intervened, he still wrote of the statue of the Virgin:

> She made the earth below seem holy ground.
> This may be superstition, weak or wild,
> But even the faintest relics of a shrine
> Of any worship wake some thoughts divine.
> Don Juan, xiii, st. 61 (1823).

Byron was always strongly attracted by the sensuous element in religious rituals. For this he may have been prepared in part by Anglicanism: 'I always took great delight in the English Cathedral service. It cannot fail to inspire every man, who feels at all, with devotion. . . .'[124] It was some such feeling as this for the concrete paraphernalia of Roman worship that lay behind the letter to his Catholic friend Moore: '. . . .I am really a great admirer of tangible religion. . . .It [Catholicism] is by far the most elegant worship, hardly excepting the Greek mythology. What with incense, pictures, statues, altars, shrines, relics, and the real presence, confession, absolution,--there is something sensible to grasp at. Besides, it leaves no possibility of doubt; for those who swallow their Deity, really and truly, in transubstantiation, can hardly find anything else otherwise than easy of digestion. I am afraid that this sounds flippant, but I don't mean it to be so; only my turn of mind is so given to taking things in the absurd point of view, that it breaks out in spite of me every now and then. Still, I do assure you that I am a very good Christian.'[125]

Fletcher, the much-maligned valet, offers interesting evidence of Byron's susceptibility to 'tangible religion.' 'I have seen my lord,' he related, 'repeatedly on meeting or passing any religious ceremonies which the Roman Catholics have in their frequent processions, while at Nivia, near Venice, dismount his horse and fall on his knees, and remain in the posture till the procession had passed; and one of his lordship's grooms, who was backward in following the example of his lordship, my lord gave a violent reproof to.'[126]

Sir Walter Scott perceived this trait in Byron during their conversations and correspondence in England, just before

---

[124] Medwin, p. 47 (1821-22).
[125] Letters, VI, 58-59 (1822).
[126] Kennedy, pp. 371-2. Fletcher dates this occurrence 1817.

an outraged public opinion drove Byron into exile. Scott
later recorded his impressions of Byron's attitude toward religious questions: 'Our sentiments agreed a good deal, except upon the subjects of religion and politics, upon neither
of which I was inclined to believe that Lord Byron entertained very fixed opinions. I remember saying to him, that
I really thought, that if he lived a few years he would alter
his sentiments. He answered, rather sharply, "I suppose you
are one of those who prophesy I will turn Methodist." I replied, "No; I don't expect your conversion to be of such an
ordinary kind. I would rather look to see you retreat upon
the Catholic faith, and distinguish yourself by the austerity
of your penances. The species of religion to which you must,
or may, one day attach yourself must exercise a strong power
on the imagination." He smiled gravely, and seemed to allow
I might be right.' [27] The evidences which Byron subsequently
gave of inclination toward the faith which, of all others,
'exercises a strong power on the imagination,' confirms the
acuteness of Scott's insight. [28]

Byron's awe of the supernatural almost amounts to
fear. An earlier chapter has considered his denial of the
reality of Hell torments as the expression of uneasiness. He
was in later years quite frank upon the subject. 'I have
often wished I had been born a Catholic,' he told Medwin.
'That Purgatory of theirs is a comfortable doctrine. I wonder
the reformers gave it up, or did not substitute something as
consolatory in its room.' [29]

Guiccioli, while depending in part upon Medwin's account, also offers independent testimony that Byron's tendency
toward Rome was in part due to his fondness for the doctrine
of Purgatory. She quotes: '"Mais le catholicisme, du moins,
offre des consolations dans les sacrements, il a surtout un
dogme consolant, qui met la rigueur de Dieu avec sa miséricorde pour des êtres doués de liberté, mais faibles: c'est
le Purgatoire. Comment le protestantisme a-t-il pu renoncer
à ce dogme si humain? Pouvoir intercéder et faire du bien
aux êtres que nous avons aimés ici-bas, ce n'est pas tout à
fait s'éloigner d'eux.". . . .C'était donc en grande partie ce
dogme en harmonie avec ses idées de la justice et de la
miséricorde de Dieu, et repoussé par le protestantisme, et.

[27]Letters, III, 412.
[28]See also Byron's letter to Miss Milbanke Sept. 26, 1812: 'As a
spectacle the Catholic is more fascinating than the Greek or the Moslem'
(Letters, III, 402). Cf. Blessington, p. 232: Byron compares the eyes of
aged persons to 'the ruined casements of the abbey or castle through which
blazed the light of tapers, and the smoke of incense offered to the Deity'
(1823). Cf. Don Juan, ii, st. 196 (1818-19): 'A devotee when soars the
Host in sight. . . .feels rapture.'
[29]Medwin, p. 51 (1821-2).

par le féroce dogmatisme de Calvin, si abhorre par Lord Byron
qui l'attirait vers le catholicisme.[30]

Another aspect of Byron's thought which had a determining influence upon his attitude toward Roman Catholicism
was his intense interest in history, and consequently his profound respect for institutions or practices which could claim
an impressive antiquity.[31] This was of a piece with his own
pride of birth, his attachment to Newstead, and the pride with
which he listed an imposing array of historical works which he
claimed to have read.[32]

Hence the attack, surprising from the pen of a political radical, upon Rousseau's disciples and the conduct of the
French Revolution:

> They made themselves a fearful monument!
> The wreck of old opinions, things which grew,
> Breathed from the birth of time: the veil they rent,
> And what behind it lay, all earth shall view.
> But good with ill they also overthrew,
> Leaving but ruins, wherewith to rebuild
> Upon the same foundation, and renew
> Dungeons and thrones, which the same hour re-fill'd
> As heretofore because ambition was self-will'd.
> Child Harold, iii, st. 72 (1816).

Perhaps this will help to explain the strange juxtaposition of ideas in the famous stanza on Gibbon:

> The other, deep and slow, exhausting thought,
> And hiving wisdom with each studious year,
> In meditation dwelt, with learning wrought,
> And shaped his weapon with an edge severe,
> Sapping a solemn creed with solemn sneer;
> The lord of irony,--that master-spell,
> Which stung his foes to wrath, which grew from fear,
> And doom'd him to the zealot's ready Hell,
> Which answers to all doubts so eloquently well.
> Childe Harold, iii, st. 107 (1816).

At one breath Byron rebukes both the 'solemn sneer'
and the zealot's ready curse--the heretic and the bigot. Such
a stanza can be fully interpreted only by recognizing that
both heresy and bigotry are dominant and recurrent themes in
Byron's poetry.

[30]Guiccioli, Lord Byron, Tome I, 209.

[31]See Letters, V, 264 (1821): Roman Catholicism 'is assuredly the
oldest of the various branches of Christianity.'

[32]A glance at the list (Moore, Chapter V) will immediately cast some
doubt upon the thoroughness with which he had read.

And here is but another evidence of Byron's unique position among his contemporaries. Although aligned with Shelley on the one hand as a champion of political reform, he
stands apart from the latter's radical indifference to the
past. On the other hand, he is distinguished from Scott, with
whom he shares an historic sense, by Scott's political conservatism. The backward glance is often associated with conservatism, because it sees, not abrupt departure from human practices and beliefs, but gradual growth out of them. In dealing
with historic fact, as with literary fact, Byron is a conservative, because his approach is from the vantage-ground of a
continuous tradition. The conservative element in his attitude toward religion is represented by his tendency toward
Rome. His radicalism appears in his forward-looking thought;
political revolution and romantic art emphasize rupture with
the past. In philosophical and religious thought, his radicalism appears in a skeptical attitude toward static modes of
belief; it is the converse of conservative attention to fixed
and authoritative tradition.

It was Byron's predilection for the left wing in politics and his love of justice that led him to champion the bill
for Catholic emancipation before the House of Lords. The
speech which he delivered shows little about his religious beliefs. He was for the moment an ordinarily devout Protestant
distinguished only by a breadth of toleration not in any way
remarkable. Even had he been apathetic toward the Catholic
religion, his innate love of justice would probably have guided
him into the same course.

He naturally takes occasion during debate to be properly sarcastic of complacent orthodoxy. Speaking of the education afforded Catholic children at that time in the Protestant Charter Schools established by the government in Ireland, he says, 'A catechism is put into their hands, consist-
ing of, I believe, forty-five pages, in which are three questions relative to the Protestant religion; one of these
queries is, "Where was the Protestant religion before Luther?"
Answer: "In the Gospel." The remaining forty-four pages and
a half regard the damnable idolatry of Papists!'

It is interesting to note what Byron at that time considered the distinctive features of Catholicism: 'We are
called together to deliberate. . . .how far a difference in
the ceremonials of worship, how far believing not too little,
but too much (the worst that can be imputed to the Catholics),
how far too much devotion to their God may incapacitate our
fellow-subjects from effectually serving their king.' Byron
believed that an excessive rather than a divergent zeal distinguished the Roman from the Protestant church. But there
is nothing in the speech which will either prove or contro-
vert the belief that Byron tended toward Rome; it shows at

most a broad sympathy which he would probably have accorded to
any minority. [33]
      Byron's approach to Catholicism did not require recon-
ciliations of the minutiae of cult. His Catholicism was never
more than incipient, and he therefore never faced the immediate prospect of participation in sacramental practices to
which, because of his early Protestant training, he was often
hostile. [34] But Byron's inclination toward Catholicism was
not the result of logical conviction. It was rather a recurrent mood in which he paid small attention to details. He
was equally capable of a perfectly devout attitude toward the
offices of the church. [35]
      Any critic who wishes to insist upon the inconsistency
of Byron's thought will find very fertile ground in his references to the Virgin Mary. But a closer attention to chronolo-
gy reveals clearly the transition of his religious attitudes
from Protestant or skeptic hostility to moments of profound
reverence. [36]
      Even before Byron had left England, he had come to an
imaginative realization of what adoration of the Virgin meant
to Catholicism:

> Darkly, sternly, and all alone,
> Minotti stood o'er the altar stone.
> Madonna's face upon him shone,
> Painted in heavenly hues above,
> With eyes of light and looks of love;
> And placed upon that holy shrine
> To fix our thoughts on things divine,

[33]Note also his statement to Dallas: 'In religion, I favour the Catholic emancipation, but do not acknowledge the Pope. . . .' (Letters, I,
172, 1808). In his note to the second canto of Childe Harold (Poetical
Works, II, pp. 206-7) Byron draws an analogy between the rigor of the English rule in Ireland and the Turks' treatment of the Greeks—'a kind of
Eastern Irish Papists. . . .And shall we then emancipate our Irish Helots?
Mahomet forbid! We should then be bad Mussulmans, and worse Christians:
at present we unite the best of both—jesuitical faith, and something not
much inferior to Turkish toleration.'
[34]See the hostility toward the sacraments in Letters, I, 173 (1808).
[35]See his letter to Moore, quoted above, on transubstantiation. Many
of his other references to the sacraments or rituals are so clearly to be
interpreted as dramatic concepts that one may well doubt their validity as
evidences of Byron's own inclinations; see Deformed Transformed, II.i.137-
142; op. cit., II.iii.376-379.
[36]Most of the jibes at the worship of Mary, or at the doctrines of virgin birth and immaculate conception, have been cited: Correspondence, I,
122 (1812); Childe Harold, i, st. 71 (1812); op. cit., ii, st. 44 (1812);
note to Waltz, v. 21 (1813); and Don Juan, xi, st. 5-6 (1822). The last
is the only hostile note later than 1813.

When pictured there, we kneeling see
Her, and the boy-God on her knee,
Smiling sweetly on each prayer
To heaven, as if to waft it there. . . .
                    Siege of Corinth, vv. 947-957 (1815).

The very famous Ave Maria passage in Don Juan[37] need
hardly be reproduced here. The admixture of pantheism and
natural religion which follows it by no means proves that
Byron's reverence was shallow. He very probably felt nothing
incongruous between nature-mysticism and the adoration of a
religious personage. Nor need the phrase

            Ave Maria! 'tis the hour of prayer!
            Ave Maria! 'tis the hour of love

be interpreted as heavenly love to redeem the passage from
incongruity. Byron was quite capable of finding in saint-
worship and in romantic love the common element of esthetic
satisfaction. The juxtaposition of Mariolatry and romantic
love is not offensive to the medieval point of view which
lingers in the Catholic faith.

From the doctrinal point of view, his rejection of
such cardinal dogmas as the vicarious atonement, the triune
nature of the Deity, and the efficacy of sacraments, were effective bars between him and belief in almost any Christian
creed. Byron knew perfectly well, however, that religious af-
filiation was almost always the result of childhood training,
and that those obstacles which lay between him and Catholic
worship would not exist for his daughter Allegra, who was being cared for by the Shelleys, if she were placed in the hands
of Catholics. His letters on the subject are extremely interesting, and not too long to reproduce in part:

        She is sometimes vain and obstinate, but always
    clean and cheerful, and as, in a year or two, I shall
    either send her to England, or put her in a Convent for
    education, these defects will be remedied as far as they
    can in human nature. But the Child shall not quit me
    again to perish of Starvation, and green fruit, or be
    taught to believe that there is no Deity.[38]

    I had no resource but to place her for a time (at a
    high pension too) in the convent of Bagna-Cavalli
    [sic] (twelve miles off), where. . . .she will, at
    least, have her learning advanced, and her morals and

[37]Canto, iii, st. 101-104. Note also the description of the niche in
which the Virgin's statue had stood at Newstead, Don Juan, xiii, st. 61.
    [38]Letters, V, 15 (1820). The Shelleys had been signally unsuccessful
in raising their own children.

religion inculcated. . . .It is, besides, my wish that
she should be a Roman Catholic, which I look upon as the
best religion, as it is assuredly the oldest of the
various branches of Christianity.[39]

I am no enemy to religion, but the contrary. As a proof,
I am educating my natural daughter a strict Catholic in
a convent of Romagna; for I think people can never have
enough of religion, if they are to have any. I incline,
myself, very much to the Catholic doctrines.[40]

I am really a great admirer of tangible religion; and
am breeding one of my daughters a Catholic, that she
may have her hands full.[41]

As far as the advantages of a conventual education
were concerned, Byron seems to have been actuated primarily by
what he considered the excellence and fullness of Catholic
discipline. He wished that Allegra might 'have her hands
full'; this is strongly reminiscent of his characterization of
Catholicism in the speech before Parliament, upon which occasion he remarked that Catholics were to be charged only with
'believing not too little, but too much,' and with having 'too
much devotion.' He believed that in the Catholic faith the
communicant was assailed by no doubt, and that he was the better for strict discipline in morals and creed. It was impossible for Byron to lay aside his own doubts and his own heritage. But the fault should be remedied in Allegra's life. She
should live as he might wish to have lived.

One of the many tragic ironies of Byron's life was
that Allegra should die in the convent where he had placed
her. The extreme agitation with which he received the news of
her death has been recounted by Guiccioli,[42] who probably had
a strong influence upon Byron's beliefs and his consequent action with regard to Allegra. Yet the traces of Guiccioli's
influence are strangely elusive. There is no documentary evidence that the Countess sought in any way to urge upon Byron
the claims of Roman Catholicism, or that his relations with
her inclined him toward Rome.

None the less it is probable that Guiccioli, more than
any other one person, brought him into a close and sympathetic
contact with Italian culture. The far-reaching effects of
continental civilization upon Byron's intellectual and poetic
development have been noted several times. Whether as an
immediate personal influence, or as the type of Latin culture,

[39]Letters, V, 264 (1821).
[40]Letters, VI, 32 (1822).
[41]Letters, VI, 38-9 (1822).
[42]Reprinted Letters, VI, 50 ff., with Moore's translation. See Moore,
p. 567, for same.

Guiccioli's ascendancy in Byron's thoughts coincides with the years in which his tendencies toward Catholicism were most strongly in evidence.

It seems perfectly possible that Byron's early hostility to 'popery' would have subsided with the access of greater experience among books and men. His predilection for historic institutions, his reverence for the concrete in worship, and his receptivity to the spectacular element in rituals would no doubt have been in evidence without Guiccioli's influence. But there is also reason to believe that Byron's intimate relations with the Gamba family stimulated him to more decisive action and to stronger statements of his incipient Catholicism.

By 'action' is to be understood his placing Allegra in the hands of Roman Catholics for her rearing; this is something far more decisive than any poetic expression of reverence for the Catholic tradition. And never, before his stay in Italy, would Byron have made the explicit statement that he considered the Roman to be 'the best religion.' It may seem paradoxical to maintain that Byron was nearest to realizing his Catholic tendencies in word and action during the years 1820 and following, since it was in the same period that his philosophical thought inclined most strongly to rationalistic skepticism. But it must be remembered that Byron's inclination toward the Roman church was not a matter of rationalistic reconciliation with dogma. It was a mood, an emotional attraction, a feeling.

Here again emerges the evidence of Byron's close relation to Romantic types of thought. His tendency toward Rome was the result of a partial surrender to the guidance of those phases of mental life which the romanticist psychology would designate as 'feeling' in distinction to knowledge and will. The romantic theory of religion,[43] asserting that religion is essentially an aspect of feeling, that is to say, a non-rational or extra-cognitive state of mind, would explain Byron's responsiveness to Catholic worship as an attitude independent of the testimony of critical reflection. This is not to say that Catholicism recommended itself to Byron because it was not rationalistic; it attracted him in spite of his rationalism. From the romanticist's point of view, doctrines and creeds seem the product of subsequent reflection upon religious feeling; and Byron's challenge to doctrinal authority is hence essentially a challenge to what he considered an accretion upon the essentials of worship. As a romanticist, he sought to ignore, albeit unsuccessfully, the teachings of doctrinal authority, as though he believed that the roots of religion lay deeper than all critical thought. Byron's philosophical speculation, like his literary criticism, was rationalistic; his literary practice was conspicuously romantic, and his religious beliefs were incipiently so.

[43] See John Baillie, The Interpretation of Religion, New York, 1928, p. 202 ff., on the romantic period of theology.

Chapter Five

C O N C L U S I O N

The torch shall be extinguish'd which hath lit
My midnight lamp--and what is writ, is writ,--
Would it were worthier!
                                        Childe Harold.

The four currents of Byron's thought outlined in the
foregoing pages are not easily brought within the confines of
a single chart. His thought did not flow in a regular course;
it swirled through a dozen channels, constantly shifting its
bars and crumbling its banks. But if the individual eddies
and cross-currents are for the moment ignored, it may be possible to describe briefly the general drift of Byron's thought.
His thoughts played constantly upon four major types
of religious or philosophical theory. All through his early
manhood, and in his intellectual maturity, he was unable to
escape the spell which the dogmas of his Calvinistic heritage
had cast upon him. Actuated by a desire to escape the torment of religious fears, and impelled, moreover, by the irrepressible activity of an inquiring mind, he experienced periods of skepticism which in Don Juan ranged from violent
hostility to traditional creeds to intense reflection upon
the problem of knowledge. Still another manifestation of his
skepticism, his devotion to the rationalistic literature of
the eighteenth century, led by easy stages from natural religion to nature-mysticism dominated by the influence of Rousseau and Shelley; finally he blended traditional naturalism
with early nineteenth-century scientific theories. In his
most mature thought some agreement might conceivably be traced
between his interest in evolutionary science and his developmental theories of knowledge; but the persistence of Calvinistic influences, evidenced in the relatively late Biblical
dramas and the vigorous attention to moral values in Don Juan,
shows that he was not approaching a systematic philosophy. His
critical reflection always suffered periods of suspension; and
during such periods his fondness for the beauty and mystery of
Catholicism took strong hold of his imagination. He was inconsistent to the last.
It would scarcely be necessary to make the point, had
not the very thorough investigation of Byron's naturalism by
Eimer led him to the conclusion that Byron approached an inward serenity of spirit due to the progressive clarification

of his convictions.[1] The opinion of most other critics is
that Byron achieved no harmony. 'He has no light,' wrote
Arnold.[2] His mental development, proceeding by accumulation
rather than by systematization, occasioned a catholicity of
interests, which, for him, precluded a nice ordering of beliefs. The shifting of his religious opinions is hence thoroughly representative of his intellectual stature.

A word might be added in explanation of the phrase,
'moral values in Don Juan.' Byron insists all through the
poem that it has a moral purpose. In almost all his works he
was constantly concerned with guilt and the associated mental
states. The heroes of his early tales were not flesh and
blood portraits, but silhouettes in black and white distinguished from each other only by their outlines. In drama
he deliberately sought to employ moral evil as the tragic
flaw. 'I must remark from Aristotle and Rymer, that the hero
of tragedy and (I add meo periculo) a tragic poem must be
guilty, to excite "terror and pity."'[3] From the first cantos
of Childe Harold to the mocking stanzas of Don Juan his poetry
has a constant refrain, that license is disabling in its consequences to those

> Whose headlong passions form their proper woes.
> And that's the moral of this composition.
> Don Juan, vi, st. 87-88.

Byron's habitual concern with good and evil has won
him the commendation of humanistic critics and has led his
champions to align him in some measure with classical art.
But it should be noted that Byron's 'persistent moral sense'
is not neo-classical; it is not the pursuit of virtue for its

---

[1]See Eimer, p. 200 ff.: 'Und doch ist dies kosmische Element in Byrons
Dichtung so deutlich. . . .dasz man darüber den Revolutionär Byron ganz
vergessen möchte. . . .man wird doch nicht verkennen, dass ein immer
stärkeres Gegengewicht innerer Ruhe und Überzeugung, eben durch die
kosmischen Anschauungen, in Byron lebendig war. . . .der Kain, oder. . . .
Himmel und Erde, verlieren durch die Erkentnis dieses Gegengewichtes. . . .
an seelischer Bedrücktheit. Sie lehren uns, noch tiefer als seine frühere
Naturdichtung, wo Byron Trost suchte, und wo er ihn fand: er hat sie nicht
nur des religiösen Stoffes wegen so gestaltet, wie sie sind. . . .So wirr
sein Spott erscheinen mag,—es liegt darunter viel von der Ruhe der
Abklärung versteckt.'

[2]Essays in Criticism, p. 198. See also More, 'Wholesome Revival of
Byron,' p. 809: '. . . .the bondage of darkness from which he never
escaped.' Elze and Mazzini concur in the view here taken, and among more
modern critics Symons (p. 261) and Calvert (p. 19), whose conclusion is
based upon an examination of Byron's critical and literary reflections.

[3]Letters, V, 284; see also Chew, Dramas, Chapter IX.

own sake. For the good life _per se_ Byron cared little; the
rub came in the consequences.

> . . . . there's Epicurus
>   And Aristippus, a material crew!
> Who to immoral courses would allure us
>   By theories quite practicable too;
> If only from the devil they would insure us,
>   How pleasant were the maxim (not quite new),
> 'Eat, drink, and love, what can the rest avail us?'
> _Don Juan_, ii, st. 207.

Byron always saw evil as an objective reality; hence
his interest in what Bishop Heber called 'the worser half of
Manicheism.'[4] His moral sense was the product of Calvinistic
training, reinforced by the practical wisdom of disillusioned
experience.

> If in the course of such a life as was
>   At once adventurous and contemplative,
> Men, who partake all passions as they pass,
>   Acquire the deep and bitter power to give
> Their images again as in a glass,
>   And in such colours that they seem to live;
> You may do right forbidding them to show 'em,
> But spoil (I think) a very pretty poem.
> _Don Juan_, iv, st. 107.

But the significance of Byron's poetry is not to be
determined by his adherence to any one school of thought. Had
Byron's search for a satisfactory body of beliefs failed only
because he followed no single path to its end upon a peak in
Darien, one might regret his want of single-mindedness. But
Byron was not intended for a prophet; his interest was in the
present, in immediate reality. 'He taught poetry to be vividly interested in all earthly things.'[5] His gropings into the
mysteries of religion and philosophy, his scientific curiosity,
and his concern with current affairs, bear the marks of an active mind but not of prophetic wisdom. Hence his spiritual
and intellectual stature is not to be reckoned by the qualities which distinguish the seer, but by its power to typify
the thought and aspirations of his contemporaries. Though he
could steal no fire from Heaven, he was not content to gather
leeches. His significance to literature was his ability to
fashion from the materials of realistic art a body of poetry
which spoke straight to the heart of liberalism.

[4] _Quarterly Review_; reprinted, _Letters_, V, 54, note 2.
[5] Symons, p. 256.

BIBLIOGRAPHY

EDITIONS OF BYRON'S WORKS

Letters and Journals of Lord Byron. Edited by R. E. Prothero
  (Lord Ernle). 6 vols. London: 1898-1901.
Lord Byron's Correspondence. Edited by John Murray. 2 vols.
  London: 1922.
The Poetical Works of Lord Byron. Edited by E. H. Coleridge.
  7 vols. London: 1905.
The Complete Poetical Works of Lord Byron. Cambridge edition.
  Edited by Paul Elmer More. 1 vol. New York: 1905.
Seventeen Letters of George Noel Gordon, Lord Byron. New
  York: 1930.
N.B. Footnotes referring to these editions employ the terms
  Letters, Correspondence, and Poetical Works for the first
  three editions respectively. The numbers of lines of the
  poems conform to the one-volume Cambridge edition, and are
  not always identical with those of the Coleridge edition.

LIST OF WORKS CITED AND OF OTHER PERTINENT STUDIES

Ackermann, Richard, Lord Byron. Heidelberg: 1901.
Arnold, Matthew, 'Preface' of Poetry of Byron. London: 1881.
  Reprinted in Essays in Criticism, Second Series. London:
  1888.
Blessington, The Countess of (Marguerite P. F. Gardiner), A
  Journal of the Conversations of Lord Byron. London: 1893.
Brandes, George, Main Currents in Nineteenth Century Litera-
  ture. Vol. IV, 'Naturalism in England.' New York: 1906.
Brooke, Stopford, 'Byron's Cain,' Hibbert Journal, XVIII
  (1919), 74-94.
Calvert, William J., Byron, Romantic Paradox. Chapel Hill:
  1935.
Chew, Samuel C., The Dramas of Lord Byron. Göttingen: 1915.
Chew, Samuel C., Byron in England. New York: 1924.
Courthope, William J., 'The Revival of Romance: Scott, Byron,
  Shelley,' The National Review, V. (1886). Reprinted in The
  Liberal Movement in English Literature, London: 1885.
Donner, J. O. E., Lord Byrons Weltanschauung. Helsingfors:
  1897.
Drinkwater, John, The Pilgrim of Eternity. New York: 1925.
Du Bos, Charles, Byron and the Need of Fatality. Translated
  by Ethel Colburn Mayne. New York: 1932.

Edgcumbe, Richard, Byron: The Last Phase. London: 1910.

Eimer, Manfred, 'Byrons Pantheismus vom Jahre 1816,' Englische Studien, XLIII, 396-425.

Eimer, Manfred, Byron und der Kosmos (in Anglistische Forschungen, XXXIV). Heidelberg: 1912.

Elze, Karl, Lord Byron. London: 1872.

Finlay, George, 'Reminiscences of Lord Byron.' In L. F. C. Stanhope's Greece in 1823 and 1824, pp. 409 ff. London: 1825.

Fuess, C. M., Lord Byron as a Satirist in Verse. New York: 1912.

Fuhrmann, Ludwig, Die Belesenheit des Jungen Byron. Berlin: 1903.

Galt, John, Life of Lord Byron. London: 1830.

Gamba, Pietro, Narrative of Lord Byron's Last Journey to Greece. London: 1825.

Gillardon, Heinrich, Shelleys Einwirkung auf Byron. Karlsruhe: 1898.

Greeff, A., 'Byrons Lucifer,' Englische Studien, XXXVI, 64 ff.

Guiccioli, Teresa G., Lord Byron Jugé par les Témoins de sa Vie. Paris: 1868.

Heber, Reginald, (A review of Byron's dramas) The Quarterly Review, XXVII (1822), 477-524.

Hobhouse, J. C. (Lord Broughton), A Journey Through Albania and Other Provinces of Turkey. London: 1813.

Hobhouse, J. C. (Lord Broughton), Recollections of a Long Life. London: 1909-1911.

Kennedy, James, Conversations on Religion with Lord Byron. London: 1830.

MacCarthy, Desmond, 'Byron: Man and Poet,' Saturday Review of Literature, VI (1930), 844-845.

Maurois, André, Byron. New York: 1930.

Mayn, Georg, Ueber Lord Byrons Heaven and Earth. Breslau: 1887.

Mayne, Ethel C., Byron. New York: 1912. Revised edition, 1 vol., New York: 1924.

Mazzini, Joseph, 'Byron and Goethe,' Life and Writings of Joseph Mazzini. Vol. VI, 61 ff. London: 1908.

Medwin, Thomas, Journal of the Conversations of Lord Byron. New York: 1824.

Messac, Régis, 'Caïn et le Probleme du Mal dans Voltaire, Byron, et Leconte de Lisle,' Revue de Littérature Compara-tive, IV (1924), 620-652.

Milbanke, Ralph (Earl of Lovelace), Astarte. London: 1921.

Moore, Thomas, The Life of Lord Byron. London: 1851.

More, Paul Elmer, 'The Wholesome Revival of Byron,' Atlantic Monthly, LXXXII (1898), 801-809.

More, Paul Elmer, 'A Note on Byron's Don Juan,' Shelburne Es-says (Third Series). New York: 1906.

Nichol, John, Byron. London: 1908.

Pönitz, Arthur, Byron und die Bibel. Berlin: 1906.

Quennell, Peter, Byron. New York: 1935.

Rebec, George, 'Byron and Morals,' International Journal of Ethics, XIV (1903), 39-54.

Richter, Helene, Lord Byron, Persönlichkeit und Werk. Halle (Saale): 1929.

Sarrazin, G., 'Byron als Nachahmer Thomsons,' Englische Studien, XVI (1892), 462 ff.

Schaffner, Alfred, Lord Byrons Cain und seine Quellen. Strassburg: 1880.

Schmidt, Otto, Rousseau und Byron. Leipzig: 1890.

Shelley, P. B., The Letters of Percy Bysshe Shelley. London: 1912.

Stanhope, L. F. C., Greece in 1823 and 1824. London: 1825. (Contains 'Reminiscences of Lord Byron' by George Finlay, p. 409 ff., and 'Sketch of Lord Byron' by Stanhope, p. 530 ff.)

Swinburne, A. C., 'Preface,' Selections from the Works of Lord Byron. London: 1866.

Symonds, J. A., 'Lord Byron' (introductory essay with Byron selection), The English Poets. Edited by T. H. Ward. Vol. IV. London: 1860.

Symons, Arthur, The Romantic Movement in English Poetry. New York: 1909.

Taine, H. A., History of English Literature. Vol. IV. New York: 1889.

Treitschke, Heinrich, 'Lord Byron und der Radicalismus,' Historische und Politische Aufsätze. I, 305 ff. Leipzig: 1903.

Trelawny, E. J., Recollections of the Last Days of Shelley and Byron. London: 1858.

Weiser, Carl, Popes Einfluss auf Byrons Jugenddichtungen. Halle: 1877.

Wenzel, G., 'Milton und Byrons Satan,' Archiv für das Studium der Neueren Sprachen und Litteraturen, LXXXIII (1889), 67-90.